THE EPIC OF
GILGAMESH

I0163673

translated by
R. Campbell Thompson

Benediction Classics

ISBN: 978-1-78943-447-7.

CONTENTS

Preface

THE Epic of Gilgamesh, written in cuneiform on Assyrian and Babylonian clay tablets, is one of the most interesting poems in the world. It is of great antiquity, and, inasmuch as a fragment of a Sumerian Deluge text is extant, it would appear to have had its origin with the Sumerians at a remote period, perhaps the fourth millennium, or even earlier. Three tablets of it exist written in Semitic Akkadian, which cannot be much later than 2,000 B.C.: half a millennium later come the remains of editions from Boghaz Keui, the Hittite capital in the heart of Asia Minor, written not only in Akkadian, but also in Hittite and another dialect. After these comes the tablet found at Ashur, the old Assyrian capital, which is anterior in date to the great editions now preserved in the British Museum, which were made in the seventh century B.C., for the Royal Library at Nineveh, one Sin-liqi-unninni being one of the editors. Finally there are small neo-Babylonian fragments representing still later editions.

In the seventh-century edition, which forms the main base of our knowledge of the poem, it was divided into twelve tablets, each containing about three hundred lines in metre. Its subject was the Legend of Gilgamesh, a composite story made up probably of different myths which had grown up at various times around the hero's name. He was one of the earliest Kings of Uruk in the South of Babylonia, and his name is found written on a tablet giving the rulers of Uruk, following in order after that of Tammuz, the god of vegetation and one of the husbands of Ishtar, who in his turn follows Lugal-banda, the tutelary god of the House of Gilgamesh. The mother of Gilgamesh was Nin-sun. According to the Epic, long ago in the old days of Babylonia, perhaps 5,000 B.C., when all the cities had their own kings, and each state rose and fell according to the ability of its ruler, Gilgamesh is holding Uruk in thrall, and the inhabitants appeal to the Gods to be relieved from his tyranny. To aid them the wild man Enkidu is created, and he, seduced by the wiles of one of the dancing girls of the Temple of Ishtar, is enticed into the great city, where at once it would appear by ancient right Gilgamesh attempts to rob him of his love. A tremendous fight ensues, and mutual admiration of each other's prowess follows, to so great an extent that the two heroes become firm friends, and determine to make an expedition together to the Forest of Cedars which is guarded by an Ogre, Humbaba, to carry off the cedar wood for the adornment of the city. They encounter Humbaba, and by the help of the Sun-god who sends the winds to their aid, capture him and cut off his head; and then, with this exploit, the goddess Ishtar, letting her eye rest on the handsome Gilgamesh, falls in love with him. But he rebuffs her proposal to wed him with contumely, and she, indignant at the insult, begs her father Anu to make a divine bull to destroy the two heroes. This bull, capable of killing three hundred men at one blast of his fiery breath, is overcome by Enkidu, who thus incurs the punishment of hybris at the hands of the gods, who decide that, although Gilgamesh may be spared, Enkidu must die. With the death of his friend, Gilgamesh in horror at the thought of similar extinction goes in search of eternal life, and after much adventuring, meets first with Siduri, a goddess who makes wine, whose philosophy of life, as she gives it him, however sensible, is evidently intended to smack of the hedonism of the bacchante. Then he meets with Ur-Shanabi the boatman of Uta-Napishtim who may perhaps have been introduced as a second philosopher to give his advice to the hero, which is now lost; conceivably he has been brought into the story because of the sails? which would have carried them over the waters of Death by means of the winds, the Breath of Life?, if Gilgamesh had not previously destroyed them with his own hand. Finally comes the meeting with Uta-Napishtim Noah who tells Gilgamesh the story of the Flood, and how the gods gave him, the one man saved, the gift of eternal life. But who can do this for Gilgamesh, who is so human as to be overcome by sleep? No, all Uta-Napishtim can do is to tell him of a plant at the bottom of the sea which will make him young again, and to obtain this plant, Gilgamesh, tying stones on his feet in the manner of Bahrein pearl-divers, dives into the water. Successful, he sets off home with his plant, but, while he is washing at a chance pool, a snake snatches it from him, and he is again frustrated of his quest, and nothing now is left him save to seek a way of summoning Enkidu back from Hades, which he tries to do by transgressing every tabu known to those who mourn for the dead. Ultimately, at the bidding of the God of the Underworld, Enkidu comes forth and pictures the sad fate of the dead in the Underworld to his friend, and on this sombre note, the tragedy ends.

Of the poetic beauty of the Epic, there is no need to speak. Expressed in a language which has perhaps the simplicity, not devoid of cumbrousness, of Hebrew rather than the flexibility of Greek, it can nevertheless describe the whole range of human emotions in the aptest language, from the love of a mother for her son to the fear of death in the primitive mind of one who has just seen his friend die; or from the anger of a woman scorned to the humour of an editor laughing in his sleeve at the ignorance of a savage.

To George Smith, one of the greatest geniuses Assyriology has produced, science owes much for the first arrangement and translations of the text of this extraordinary poem: indeed, it was for this Epic that he sacrificed his life, for actually it was the discovery of the Deluge Tablet in the British Museum Collections which led the *Daily Telegraph* to subscribe so generously for the re-opening of the diggings in the hope of further finds at Kouyunjik Nineveh, in conducting which he died all too early in 1876. Sir Henry Rawlinson and Professor Pinches played no small part in the reconstruction and publication of at least two of the tablets, and to their labours in this field must be added the ingenuity of Professor Sayce and the solid acumen of Dr. L. W King. In America to Professor Haupt is owed the first complete edition of the texts, very accurately copied, and later on the editions of two early Babylonian texts were edited by Langdon, Clay and Jastrow: among German publications must be mentioned the translations of Jensen and Ungnad, with the edition of an Old Babylonian tablet by Meissner. The Boghaz Keui texts have been edited by Weidner, Friedrich, and Ungnad. It would be superfluous to say how much I am indebted to the labours of all these scholars.

The present version is based on a fresh collation of the original tablets in the British Museum, the results of which I propose to publish shortly in a critical edition of both text and translation. It will be seen that I have departed from the accepted order of several of the fragments of which the position in the Epic is problematical. An examination of numerous fragments of tablets of a religious nature has naturally led to the discovery of duplicates and joins, some of which will be apparent in the present text. For their great liberality in granting me facilities to copy and collate these valuable tablets I have to express my heartiest thanks to the Trustees of the British Museum, and the Director, Sir Frederick Kenyon. To my friends Dr. H. R. Hall, and Messrs. Sidney Smith and C. J. Gadd of the British Museum, I am greatly indebted for much help in forwarding the work: and to Sir John Miles, Fellow of Merton College, Oxford, I owe many shrewd suggestions.

R. CAMPBELL THOMPSON.

NINEVEH,
CHRISTMAS, 1927.

The First Tablet:
Of the Tyranny of Gilgamesh, and the
Creation of Enkidu

Column I.

(The Argument).

He who the heart of all matters hath proven let him teach the nation,

He who all knowledge possesseth, therein shall he school all the people,
He shall his wisdom impart and so shall they share it together.
Gilgamesh —he was the Master of wisdom, with knowledge of all things,
He 'twas discovered the secret conceal'd . . . .
Aye, handed down the tradition relating to things prediluvian,
Went on a journey afar, all aweary and worn with his toiling,
Graved on a table of stone all the travail.
Of Uruk, the high-wall'd,
He it was built up the ramparts; and he it was clamp'd the foundation,
Like unto brass, of E-Anna , the sacred, the treasury hallow'd,
Strengthen'd its base to grant wayleave to no one . . . . . .
. . . . . the threshold which from of old . . . . . .
. . . . . E-Anna . . . .
. . . . to grant wayleave to no one . . . .

(About thirty lines wanting. The description of Gilgamesh runs on to the beginning of the next Column).

Column II.

Two-thirds of him are divine, and one-third of him human, . . .

The form of his body . . . .

He hath forced to take . . . .

(Gap of about three lines).

(The Plaint of Uruk(?) to the gods against the tyrant Gilgamesh)

". . . . . of Uruk 'tis he who hath taken,
. . . . while tow'reth his crest like an aurochs,

Ne'er hath the shock of his weapons its peer; are driven his fellows
Into the toils , while cow'd are the heroes of Uruk un- . . . . .
Gilgamesh leaveth no son to his father, his arrogance swelling
Each day and night; aye, he is the shepherd of Uruk, the high-wall'd,
He is our shepherd . . . . masterful, dominant, subtle . . .
Gilgamesh leaveth no maid to her mother, nor daughter to hero,
Nay, nor a spouse to a husband"
And so, to th' appeal of their wailing
Gave ear th' Immortals: the gods of high heaven address'd the god Anu,
Him who was Seigneur of Uruk : "'Tis thou a son hast begotten,
Aye, in sooth, all tyrannous, while tow'reth his crest like an aurochs,
Ne'er hath the shock of his weapons its peer; are driven his fellows
Into the toils, awhile cow'd are the heroes of Uruk un- . . . . .
Gilgamesh leaveth no son to his father, his arrogance swelling
Each day and night; aye, he is the shepherd of Uruk, the high-wall'd,
He is their shepherd . . . masterful, dominant, subtle . . .
Gilgamesh leaveth no maid to her mother, nor daughter to hero,
Nay, nor a spouse to a husband."
And so, to th' appeal of their wailing
 Anu gave ear, call'd the lady Aruru : "'Twas thou, O Aruru,
Madest primeval seed of mankind: do now make its fellow,
So that he happen on Gilgamesh, yea, on the day of his pleasure,
So that they strive with each other, and he unto Uruk give surcease."

(The Creation of Enkidu).

So when the goddess Aruru heard this, in her mind she imagined
Straightway, this Concept of Anu, and, washing her hands, then Aruru
Finger'd some clay, on the desert she moulded it: thus on the desert
Enkidu made she, a warrior, as he were born and begotten,
Yea, of Ninurta the double, and put forth the whole of his body
Hair: in the way of a woman he snooded his locks in a fillet;
Sprouted luxuriant growth of his hair-like the awns of the barley,
Nor knew he people nor land; he was clad in a garb like Sumuqan .

E'en with gazelles did he pasture on herbage, along with the cattle
Drank he his fill, with the beasts did his heart delight at the water.

(The Encounter of Enkidu with the Hunter).

Then did a hunter, a trapper, come face to face with this fellow,
Came on him one, two, three days, at the place where the beasts drank their water;
Sooth, when the hunter espied him, his face o'ermantled with terror,
He and his cattle went unto his steading, dismay'd and affrighted,
Crying aloud, distress'd in, his heart, and his face overclouded,
. . . . woe in his belly . . . .

Aye, and his face was the same as of one who hath gone a far journey.

Column III.

Open'd his mouth then the hunter, and spake, addressing his father:
"Father, there is a great fellow come forth from out of the mountains,
O, but his strength is the greatest the length and breadth of the country,
Like to a double of Anu's own self his strength is enormous,
Ever he rangeth at large o'er the mountains, and ever with cattle
Grazeth on herbage and ever he setteth his foot to the water,
So that I fear to approach him. The pits which I myself hollow'd
With mine own hands hath he fill'd in again, and the traps of my setting
Torn up, and out of my clutches hath holpen escape all the cattle,
Beasts of the desert: to work at my fieldcraft he will not allow me."

Open'd his mouth then his father, and spake, addressing the hunter:
"Gilgamesh dwelleth in Uruk, my son, whom no one hath vanquish'd,
 Nay, but 'tis his strength is greatest the length and breadth of the country
Like to a double of Anu's own self, his strength is enormous,
 Go, set thy face towards Uruk: and when he hears of a monster,
 He will say 'Go, O hunter, a courtesan-girl, a hetaera

Take with thee . . . . like a strong one;
When he the cattle shall gather again to the place of their drinking,
So shall she put off her mantle the charm of her beauty revealing;
Then shall he spy her, and sooth will embrace her, and thenceforth
his cattle,
Which in his very own deserts were rear'd, will straightway deny him.'"

(How Gilgamesh first heard of Enkidu).

Unto the rede of his father the hunter hath hearken'd, and straightway
He will away unto Gilgamesh .
Taking the road towards Uruk
Turn'd he his steps, and to Gilgamesh came, his speech thus addressing:
Saying: "There is a great fellow come forth from out of the mountains,
O, but his strength is the greatest, the length and breadth of the country,
Like to a double of Anu's own self his strength is enormous,
Ever he rangeth at large o'er the mountains, and ever with cattle
Grazeth on herbage, and ever he setteth his foot to the water,
So that I fear to approach him . The pits which I myself hollow'd
With mine own hands hath he fill'd in again, and the traps of my setting
Torn up, and out of my clutches hath holpen escape all the cattle,
Beasts of the desert: to work at my fieldcraft he will not allow me."
Gilgamesh unto him, unto the hunter made answer in this wise:
"Go, good my hunter, take with thee a courtesan-girl, a hetaera,
When he the cattle shall gather again to the place of their drinking,

So shall she put off her mantle, the charm of her beauty revealing,
Then shall he spy her, and sooth will embrace her, and thenceforth his cattle
Which in his very own deserts were rear'd will straightway deny him. "

(The Seduction of Enkidu).

Forth went the hunter, took with him a courtesan-girl, a hetaera,
So did they start on their travels, went forth on their journey together,
Aye, at the term of three days arrived at the pleasaunce appointed.
Sate they down in their ambush, the hunter and the hetaera,
One day, two days they sat by the place where the beasts drank their water.

Then at last came the cattle to take their fill in their drinking.

Column IV.

Thither the animals came that their hearts might delight in the water,
Aye, there was Enkidu also, he whom the mountains had gender'd,
E'en with gazelles did he pasture on herbage, along with the cattle
Drank he his fill , with the beasts did his heart delight at the water,
So beheld him the courtesan-girl, the lusty great fellow,
O but a monster all savage from out of the depths of the desert!
"'Tis he, O girl! O, discover thy beauty, thy comeliness shew him,
So that thy loveliness he may possess—O, in no wise be bashful,
Ravish the soul of him—certes, as soon as his eye on thee falleth,
He, forsooth, will approach thee, and thou—O, loosen thy mantle,
So that he clasp thee, and then with the wiles of a woman shalt ply him;
Wherefore his animals, bred in his desert, will straightway deny him,
Since to his breast he hath held thee."
The girl, displaying her bosom,
Shew'd him her comeliness, yea so that he of her beauty possess'd him,
Bashful she was not, but ravish'd the soul of him, loosing her mantle,
So that he clasp'd her, and then with the wiles of a woman she plied him,
Holding her unto his breast.
'Twas thus that Enkidu dallied
Six days, aye seven nights, with the courtesan-girl in his mating.

(How Enkidu was inveigled into Uruk to fight with Gilgamesh.)

Sated at length with her charms, he turn'd his face to his cattle,

O the gazelles, how they scamper'd away, as soon as they saw him!
Him, yea, Enkidu,—fled from his presence the beasts of the desert!
Enkidu losing his innocence —so, when the cattle fled from him,
Failed his knees, and he
 slack'd in his running, not as aforetime:
Natheless he thus hath attain'd his full growth and hath broaden'd his wisdom.
Sat he again at the feet of the woman, the woman his features

Scanning, and, while she was speaking, his ears heard the words she was saying:
"Comely thou art, e'en like to a god, O Enkidu, shalt be,
Why with the beasts of the field dost thou ever range over the desert?
Up! for I'll lead thee to Uruk, the high-wall'd—in sooth, to the Temple
Sacred, the dwelling of Anu and Ishtar, where, highest in power,
Gilgamesh is, and prevaileth o'er men like an aurochs."

Her counsel
E'en as she spake it found favour, for conscious he was of his longing
Some companion to seek; so unto the courtesan spake he :
"Up, then, O girl, to the Temple, the holy and sacred, invite me,
 Me, to the dwelling of Anu and Ishtar, where, highest in power,
Gilgamesh is, and prevaileth o'er men like an aurochs—for I, too,

       Column V.

I, I will summon him, challenging boldly and crying through Uruk,
'I too, am mighty!' Nay, I, forsooth I, will e'en destiny alter—
Truly, 'tis he who is born in the desert whose vigour is greatest!
. . . . I will please thee,
. . . . whatever there be, that would I know."
"Enkidu, come then to Uruk, the high-wall'd, where people array them
Gorgeous in festal attire, and each day the day is a revel,
Eunuch-priests clashing their cymbals, and dancing-girls . . . . .
. . . flown with their wantoning, gleeful, and keeping the nobles
Out of their beds ! Nay, Enkidu, joy in thy life to its fullest
Thou shalt taste—forsooth will I shew thee a man who is happy,
Gilgamesh! View him, O look on his face, how comely his manhood!
Dower'd with lustiness is he, the whole of his body with power
Brimming, his vigour is stronger than thine, all day and night restless!
Enkidu, temper thine arrogance—Gilgamesh, loveth him Shamash,
Anu, and Enlil , and Ea have dower'd his wisdom with largesse.

       (How Gilgamesh dreamt of Enkidu).

Sooth, or ever from out of thy mountains thou camest, in Uruk
 Gilgamesh thee had beheld in a dream; so, Gilgamesh coming
Spake to his mother, the dream to reveal.
'O my mother, a vision
Which I beheld in my night-time. Behold, there were stars of the heavens,
When something like unto Anu's own self fell down on my shoulders,
 Ah, though I heaved him, he was o'erstrong for me, and though his grapple
Loosed I, I was unable to shake him from off me: and now, all the meanwhile,
People from Uruk were standing about him , the artisans pressing.

On him behind, while throng'd him the heroes; my very companions
Kissing his feet; I, I to my breast like a woman did hold him,

Then I presented him low at thy feet, that as mine own equal.
Thou might'st account him.'
 She who knoweth all wisdom thus to her Seigneur she answer'd,
She who knoweth all wisdom, to Gilgamesh thus did she answer:
'Lo, by the stars of the heavens are represented thy comrades,
That which was like unto Anu's own self, which fell on thy shoulders,
Which thou didst heave, but he was, o'erstrong for thee, aye, though his grapple
Thou didst unloose, but to shake him from off thee thou wert un able,
So didst present him low at my feet, that as thine own equal
I might account him—and thou to thy breast like a woman didst hold him:

Column VI.

This is a stoutheart, a friend, one ready to stand by a comrade,
One whose strength is the greatest, the length and breadth of the country,
Like to a double of Anu's own self his strength is enormous.
Now, since thou to thy breast didst hold him the way of a woman,
This is a sign that thou art the one he will never abandon:
This of thy dream is the meaning.'
Again he spake to his mother,
'Mother, a second dream did I see: Into Uruk, the high-wall'd,
Hurtled an axe, and they gather'd about it: the meanwhile, from Uruk
People were standing about it, the people all thronging before it,
Artisans pressing behind it, while I at thy feet did present it,
I, like a woman I held it to me that thou might'st account it,
As mine own equal.'
She the all-wise, who knoweth all wisdom, thus answer'd her offspring,
She the all-wise who knoweth all wisdom, to Gilgamesh answer'd:
'Lo, that Axe thou didst see is a Man; like a woman didst hold him,
Unto thy breast, that as thine own equal I might account him,
This is a stoutheart, a friend, one ready to stand by a comrade,
One whose strength is the greatest the length and breadth of the country,
Like to a double of Anu's own self, his strength is enormous.'
Gilgamesh open'd his mouth, and addressing his mother, thus spake he:
            'Though great danger befall, a friend shall I have . . .'

*(The Assyrian Edition of the seventh century has three more lines on the First Tablet,
which correspond with Column II, l. 3 of the Second Tablet of the Old Babylonian
Edition. This latter has already begun with the episode of the two dreams, approxi-
mately Column V, l. 24 of the Assyrian First Tablet, and the text is so similar in
both that I have not repeated it here. The Old Babylonian Edition here takes up the
story, repeating one or two details).*

The Second Tablet:
Of the Meeting of Gilgamesh and Enkidu

Column II.

While Gilgamesh thus is the vision revealing
Enkidu sitteth before the hetaera, and she displaying her bosom,
Shewing her beauty, the place of his birth he forgetteth.
So Enkidu dallied
Thus for six days, seven nights, with the courtesan-girl in his mating.
Broke into speech then, the nymph, and thus unto Enkidu spake she:
"Yea, as I view thee, e'en like a god, O Enkidu, shalt be,
Why with the beasts of the field dost thou ever range over the desert?
Up, for I'll lead thee to Uruk broad-marketed, aye, to the Temple
Sacred, the dwelling of Anu—O Enkidu, come, that I guide thee,
Unto E-Anna, the dwelling of Anu, where Gilgamesh liveth,
He, the supreme of creation; and thou, aye, thou wilt embrace him
Like to a woman, and e'en as thyself thou shalt love him.
O, rouse thee
Up from the ground—'tis a shepherd's bed only."
Her utterance heard he,
Welcomed her rede: the advice of the woman struck home in his bosom.
She one garment took off wherewith she might clothe him: the other
She herself wore, and so taking her hand like a brother she led him
Thus to the booths of the shepherds, the place of the sheepfolds. The shepherds
Gatherd at sight of him

Gap of four or five lines.

Column III.

(How the Hetaera schooled Enkidu).

He in the past of the milk of the wild things to suck was accustom'd!
Bread which she set before him he broke, but he gazed and he stared:
Enkidu bread did not know how to eat, nor had he the knowledge

Mead how to quaff!
 Then the woman made answer, to Enkidu speaking,
"Enkidu, taste of the bread, for of life 'tis; forsooth, the essential,
Drink thou, too, of the mead, 'tis the wonted use of the country."
Enkidu ate of the bread, aye, ate until he was gorged,
Drank of the mead seven bumpers; his spirits rose, and, exultant,
Glad was his heart, and cheerful his face: himself was he rubbing,
Oil on the hair of his body anointed: and thus became human.
Donn'd he a garment to be like a man , and taking his weapon,
Hunted the lions, which harried the shepherds o' nights: and the jackals
Caught he. So he, having mastered the lions, the shepherds slept soundly .
Enkidu—he was their warden—becometh a man of full vigour.
Now is one of the heroes speaking to Gilgamesh . . . .

> *(About thirteen lines are missing, a gap in which a sinister figure has evidently appeared, sent evidently by Gilgamesh to learn the meaning of the arrival of the strangers in Uruk. Enkidu sees him and speaks).*

Column IV.

Then while he pleasured, he lifted his eyes, and, observing the fellow,
Spake he unto the woman: "O doxy, bring me this fellow,
Why hath he come? I would know his intention."
 The woman the fellow

Call'd that he come to him, that he might see him: "O, why art thou seeking,
Sir? Pray, which is the way to thy rest-house?"
 The man spake, addressing

Enkidu: "You to the House of Community Gilgamesh calleth,
This is the custom of men, and a homage too to the great ones:

Come, then, and heap up the offerings such as are due to the city,
Come, on behalf of the common weal bring in the food of the city.
'Tis for the king of broad-marketed Uruk to look on thy greeting,
Gilgamesh, king of broad-marketed Uruk to look on thy greeting;
First doth he mate with the woman allotted by fate, and then after
Speak by the counsel of god, and so from the shape of the omens
Utter the rede of his destiny."
 So at the words of the fellow

Went they before him.

> *(Gap of about nine lines.)*

Column V.

(The Entry of Enkidu into Uruk.)

Enkidu going in front, with the courtesan coming behind him,
Enter'd broad-marketed Uruk; the populace gather'd behind him,
Then, as he stopp'd in the street of broad-marketed Uruk, the people
Thronging, behind him exclaim'd "Of a truth, like to Gilgamesh is he,
Shorter in stature a trifle, his composition is stronger.
. . . . once like a weakling baby he *suck'd* the milk of the wild things!
Ever the bread-cakes in Uruk give glorious climax to manhood!
He a mere savage becometh a hero of proper appearance,
Now unto Gilgamesh, god-like, his composition is equal."

(How Enkidu fought with Gilgamesh for the Hetaera.)

Strewn is the couch for the love-rites, and Gilgamesh now in the night-time
Cometh to sleep, to delight in the woman : but Enkidu, coming
There in the highway, doth block up the passage to Gilgamesh, threat'ning
He with his strength . . . . .

(Gap of seven or eight lines).

Column VI.

Gilgamesh . . . behind him . . . .
Burgeon'd his rage, and he rush'd to attack him: they met in the highway.
Enkidu barr'd up the door with his foot, and to Gilgamesh entry—15.Would not
concede: they grappled and snorted like bulls, and the threshold
Shatter'd: the very wall quiver'd as Gilgamesh , Enkidu grappled,
Snorting like bulls, and the threshold they shatter'd, the very wall quiver'd.

(The Birth of Friendship).

Gilgamesh bent his leg to the ground: so his fury abated,
Aye, and his ardour was quell'd: so soon as was quelled his ardour,
Enkidu thus unto Gilgamesh spake: "Of a truth, did thy mother
Bear thee as one, and one only: that choicest cow of the steer-folds,
Nin-sun exalted thy head above heroes, and Enlil hath dower'd
Thee with the kingship o'er men."

The Third Tablet:
The Expedition to the Forest of Cedars Against Humbaba

(About a column and a half of the beginning of the Old Babylonian version on the Yale tablet are so broken that almost all the text is lost. Gilgamesh and Enkidu have now become devoted friends, thus strangely stultifying the purpose for which Enkidu was created, and now is set afoot the great expedition against the famous Cedar Forest guarded by the Ogre Humbaba. The courtesan has now for a brief space left the scene, having deserted Enkidu, much to his sorrow. The mutilated Assyrian Version gives a hint that the mother of Gilgamesh is now describing the fight to one of her ladies(?) Rishat-Nin . . . and where her recital becomes connected the story runs thus).

Column II.

(The Tale of the Fight).

"He lifted up his foot, to the door . . . .
 They raged furiously . . . .
Enkidu hath not his equal . . . unkempt is the hair . . .
Aye he was born in the desert, and no one his presence can equal."

(Enkidu's sorrow at the loss of his Love).

Enkidu there as he stood gave ear to his utterance, grieving
Sitting in sorrow: his eyes fill'd with tears, and his arms lost their power,
Slack'd was his bodily vigour. Each claspd the hand of the other.
Holding like brothers their grip . . . and to Gilgamesh Enkidu answer'd:
"Friend, 'tis my darling hath circled her arms round my neck to farewell me ,
Wherefore my arms lose their power, my bodily vigour is slacken 'd."

(The Ambition of Gilgamesh).

Gilgamesh open'd his mouth, and to Enkidu spake he in this wise:

Column III.

(Gap of about two lines)

"I, O my friend, am determined to go to the Forest of Cedars,
Aye and Humbaba the Fierce will o'ercome and destroy what is evil
Then will I cut down the Cedar . . . . ."
Enkidu open'd his mouth, and to Gilgamesh spake he in this wise,
"Know, then, my friend, what time I was roaming with kine in the mountains
I for a distance of two hours' march from the skirts of the Forest
Into its depths would go down. Humbaba—his roar was a whirlwind,
Flame in his jaws, and his very breath Death! O, why hast desired
This to accomplish? To meet with Humbaba were conflict unequall'd."
Gilgamesh open'd his mouth and to Enkidu spake he in this wise:
"Tis that I need the rich yield of its mountains I go to the Forest" . . . .

(Seven mutilated lines continuing the speech of Gilgamesh, and mentioning "the dwelling [of the gods?]" (of the beginning of the Fifth Tablet), and "the axe," for cutting down the Cedars).

Enkidu open'd his mouth and to Gilgamesh spake he in this wise:
"But when we go to the Forest of Cedars . . . its guard is a Fighter,
Strong, never sleeping, O Gilgamesh . . . . . .

(Three mutilated lines, apparently explaining the powers which Shamash (?), the Sun-god, and Adad, the Storm-god, have bestow'd on Humbaba).

Column IV.

So that he safeguard the Forest of Cedars a terror to mortals
Him hath Enlil appointed—Humbaba, his roar is a whirlwind,
Flame in his jaws, and his very breath Death! Aye, if he in the Forest.
Hear but a tread on the road—'Who is this come down to his Forest?'
So that he safeguard the Forest of Cedars, a terror to mortals,
Him hath Enlil appointed, and fell hap will seize him who cometh
Down to his Forest."

Gilgamesh open'd his mouth and to Enkidu spake he in this wise:
"Who, O my friend, is unconquer'd by death? A divinity, certes,
Liveth for aye in the daylight, but mortals—their days are all number'd,
All that they do is but wind—But to thee, now death thou art dreading,
Proffereth nothing of substance thy courage—I, I'll be thy va ward!
'Tis thine own mouth shall tell thou didst fear the onslaught of battle,
I, forsooth, if I should fall, my name will have stablish'd for ever.
Gilgamesh 'twas, who fought with Humbaba, the Fierce!
In the future,
After my children are born to my house, and climb up thee, saying:
'Tell to us all that thou knowest' . . . . . .

(Four lines mutilated).

Yea, when thou speakest in this wise, thou grievest my heart for the Cedar

I am determined to fell, that I may gain fame everlasting.

(The Weapons are cast for the Expedition).

Now, O my friend, my charge to the craftsmen I fain would deliver,
So that they cast in our presence our weapons."
The charge they deliver'd

Unto the craftsmen: the mould did the workmen prepare, and the axes
Monstrous they cast: yea, the celts did they cast, each weighing three talents;
Glaives, too, monstrous they cast, with hilts each weighing two talents,
Blades, thirty manas to each, corresponding to fit them: the inlay,
Gold thirty manas each sword: so were Gilgamesh , Enkidu laden
Each with ten talents.

(Gilgamesh takes counsel with the Elders).

And now in the Seven Bolt Portal of Uruk
Hearing the bruit did the artisans gather, assembled the people ,
There in the streets of broad-marketed Uruk, in Gilgamesh' honour ,
So did the Elders of Uruk broad-marketed take seat before him.
Gilgamesh spake thus: "O Elders of Uruk broad-marketed, hear me!
I go against Humbaba, the Fierce, who shall say, when he heareth ,

Column V.

'Ah, let me look on this Gilgamesh, he of whom people are speaking,
He with whose fame the countries are fill'd'—'Tis I will o'erwhelm him,
There in the Forest of Cedars—I'll make the land hear it
How like a giant the Scion of Uruk is—yea, for the Cedars
I am determined to fell, that I may gain fame everlasting."
Gilgamesh thus did the Elders of Uruk broad-marketed answer:
"Gilgamesh, 'tis thou art young, that thy valour o'ermuch doth uplift thee,
Nor dost thou know to the full what thou dost seek to accomplish.
Unto our ears hath it come of Humbaba, his likeness is twofold.
15.Who of free will then would seek to oppose in encounter his weapons?
Who for a distance of two hours' march from the skirts of the Forest
Unto its depths would go down? Humbaba, his roar is a whirlwind,
Flame in his jaws, and his very breath Death! O, why hast desired.
This to accomplish? To meet with Humbaba were conflict unequall'd."
Gilgamesh unto the rede of his counsellors hearken'd and ponder'd,
Cried to his friend: "Now, indeed, O my fried, will I thus voice opinion.
I forsooth dread him, and yet to the depths of the Forest I'll take me . ."

(About seven lines mutilated or missing in which the Elders bless Gilgamesh in fare-well).

" . . . . may thy god so protect thee,

Bringing thee back safe and sound to the walls of broad-marketed Uruk."
Gilgamesh knelt before Shamash a word in his presence to utter:
"Here I present myself, Shamash, to lift up my hands in entreaty,
O that hereafter my life may be spared, to the ramparts of Uruk
Bring me again: spread thine aegis upon me ."
And Shamash made answer,
Speaking his oracle . . . .

(About six lines mutilated or missing).

Column VI.

Tears adown Gilgamesh' cheeks were now streaming: "A road I have never
Traversed I go, on a passage I know not, but if I be spared
So in content will I come and will pay thee due meed of thy homage."

(Two mutilated lines with the words "on seats" and "his equipment.")

Monstrous the axes they brought, they deliver'd the bow and the quiver
Into his hand; so taking a celt, he slung on his quiver,
Grasping another celt he fasten'd his glaive to his baldrick.
But, or ever the twain had set forth on their journey, they offer'd
Gifts to the Sun-god, that home he might bring them to Uruk in safety.

(The Departure of the two Heroes).

Now do the Elders farewell him with blessings, to Gilgamesh giving
Counsel concerning the road: "O Gilgamesh, to thine own power
Trust not alone; but at least let thy road be traversed before thee,
Guard thou thy person; let Enkidu go before thee as vaward.
Aye, for 'twas he hath discover'd the way, the road he hath travell'd.
Sooth, of the Forest the passes are all under sway of Humbaba,
Yea, he who goeth as vaward is able to safeguard a comrade,
O that the Sun-god may grant thee success to attain thine ambition,
O that he grant that thine eyes see consummate the words of thy utt'rance
O that he level the path that is block'd, cleave a road for thy treading,
Cleave, too, the berg for thy foot! May the god Lugal-banda
Bring in thy night-time a message to thee, with which shalt be gladden'd,
So that it help thine ambition , for, like a boy thine ambition
On the o'erthrow of Humbaba thou fixest, as thou hast settled.

Wash, then, thy feet : when thou haltest , shalt hollow a pool, so that ever
Pure be the water within thy skin-bottle, aye, cool be the water
Unto the Sun-god thou pourest, and thus shalt remind Lugal-banda."
Enkidu open'd his mouth, and spake unto Gilgamesh, saying:
"Gilgamesh, art thou in truth full equal to making this foray?
Let not thy heart be afraid; trust me."
 On his shoulder his mantle

Drew he, and now on the road to Humbaba they set forth together.

> *(Five lines mutilated; the two heroes meet a man who sets them on their way).*

" . . . they went with me . . . tell you . . in joy of heart."
So when he heard this his word, the man on his way did direct him:
"Gilgamesh, go, . . . let thy brother precede thee . . . and in thine ambition.
O that the Sun-god may shew thee success!"

> *(The Old Babylonian Version breaks off after three more fragmentary lines. The fol-
> lowing is the Assyrian Version of Column VI, l. 21, and onwards of the preceding
> text. It marks the beginning of the Third Tablet in the Assyrian Version, opening
> with the episode of the conclave of the Elders).*

"Gilgamesh, put not thy faith in the strength of thine own person solely,
Quench'd be thy wishes to trusting? o'ermuch in thy shrewdness in smiting.
Sooth, he who goeth as vaward is able to safeguard a comrade,
He who doth know how to guide hath guarded his friend; so before thee,
Do thou let Enkidu go, for 'tis he to the Forest of Cedars
Knoweth the road: 'tis he lusteth for battle, and threateneth combat.
Enkidu—he would watch over a friend, would safeguard a comrade,
Aye, such an one would deliver his person from out of the pitfalls.
We, O King, in our conclave have paid deep heed to thy welfare,
Thou, O King, in return with an equal heed shalt requite us."
Gilgamesh open'd his mouth, and spake unto Enkidu, saying:
"Unto the Palace of Splendour, O friend, come, let us betake us,
Unto the presence of Nin-sun, the glorious Queen, aye to Nin-sun,
Wisest of all clever women, all-knowing; a well-devised pathway
She will prescribe for our feet."

Clasp'd they their hands, each to each, and went to the Palace of Splendour,
Gilgamesh , Enkidu. Unto the glorious Queen, aye to Nin-sun
Gilgamesh came, and he enter'd in unto the presence of Nin-sun:
"Nin-sun, O fain would I tell thee how I a far journey am going,
Unto the home of Humbaba to counter a warfare I know not,
Follow a road which I know not, aye from the time of my starting,
Till my return, until I arrive at the Forest of Cedars,
Till I o'erthrow Humbaba, the Fierce, and destroy from the country.
All that the Sun-god abhorreth of evil" . . . .

> *(The rest of the speech of Gilgamesh is lost until the end of the Column, where we find
> him still addressing his mother, and apparently asking that she shall garb herself in fes-
> tal attire to beg a favour of the Sun-god).*

" . . . garb thyself; . . . in thy presence.
So to her offspring, to Gilgamesh Nin-sun gave ear . . . . -ly,

Column II.

Enter'd her chamber . . . and deck'd herself with the flowers of *Tulal*,
Put on the festal garb of her body . . . .
Put on the festal garb of her bosom . . ., her head with a circlet
Crown'd, and . . . the ground *ipirani* .
Climb'd she the stairway, ascended the roof, and the parapet mounted,
Offer'd her incense to Shamash, her sacrifice offer'd to Shamash,
Then towards Shamash her hands she uplifted in orison saying:
"Why didst thou give this restlessness of spirit
With which didst dower Gilgamesh, my son?
That now thou touchest him, and straight he starteth
A journey far to where Humbaba dwelleth,
To counter warfare which he knoweth not,
Follow a pathway which he knoweth not,
Aye, from the very day on which he starteth,
Till he return, till to the Cedar Forest
He reach; till he o'erthrow the fierce Humbaba,
And from the land destroy all evil things
Which thou abhor'st; the day which thou hast set
As term, of that strong man who feareth thee,
May Aa , thy bride, be thy remembrancer.
He the night-watches . . . . . ."

> *(Columns III, IV, and V are much mutilated. There is the remnant of a passage in*
> *Assyrian, corresponding to the Third Tablet of the Old Babylonian Version, Column*
> *III, 15, which gives Enkidu's speech about "the mountains," "the cattle of the field,"*
> *and how "he waited": then follows another fragment with a mention of the "corpse" [of*
> *Humbaba] and of the Anunnaki (the Spirits of Heaven), and a repetition of the line*
> *"that strong man (who) feareth [thee] ." Then a reference to "the journey" until [Gilga-*
> *mesh shall have overthrown the fierce Humbaba], be it after an interval of days,*
> *months, or years; and another fragment probably part of the previous text, where some-*
> *one "heaps up incense"[to a god], and Enkidu again speaks with someone, but the*
> *mutilated text does not allow us much light on its connection, and although there is an-*
> *other fragment, the connection again is not obvious. The last column is a repetition of*
> *what the Elders said to Gilgamesh):*

"Aye, such an one would deliver his person from out of the pitfalls.
We, O King, in our conclave have paid deep heed to thy welfare,
Now, O King, in thy turn with an equal heed shalt requite us."
Enkidu open'd his mouth and spake unto Gilgamesh, saying:
"Turn, O my friend . . . . a road not . . . ."

The Fourth Tablet:
The Arrival at the Gate of the Forest

(Of Column I about ll. 1-36 are mutilated or missing, there being actually the beginnings of only sixteen lines. When the text becomes connected the heroes have reached the Gate of the Forest).

Column I.

(Enkidu addresses the Gate).

Enkidu lifted his eyes . . . and spake with the Gate as 't were human:
"O thou Gate of the Forest without understanding? . . .
Sentience which thou hast not, ...

I for full forty leagues have admired thy wonderful timber,
Aye, till I sighted the towering Cedar . . . .
O but thy wood hath no peer in the country . . .
Six *gar* thy height, and two *gar* thy breadth . . .
Sooth, but thy stanchion, thy socket, thy pivot, thy lock, and thy shutter,
All of them must have been fashion'd for thee in the City of Nippur!
O, if I had but known, O Gate, that this was thy grandeur,
This, too, the grace of thy structure, then either an axe had I lifted
Or I had . . . or bound together . . . ."

> *(Of the next Column remains a fragment, and that only presumed to belong to one of the above fragments from its appearance, which speaks of terror, a dream, and sorrow: "let me pray the gods . . . . may thy? god be . . . the father of the gods." Again, of the third Column there is only a small portion left of the right half (this fragment, too, being also presumed to belong to the same tablet as that above-mentioned), speaking of Gilgamesh, the Forest, and Enkidu. The fourth Column is entirely lost. Of Column V the latter part survives, in this case without any uncertainty. After a few broken lines it runs as follows, the first speaker being probably Enkidu, and the scene the Gate of the Forest):*

". . . O, haste thee, withstand him, he will not pursue thee,
We will go on down into the wood not daunted, together .

. . . Thou shall put on seven garments ..
. . . putting on, and six . . . . . . "
He like a mighty wild bull . . .
Flung he the Portal afar, and his mouth was fill'd with his challenge,
Cried to the Guard of the Forest: "Up . . . !
'Tis I will challenge Humbaba like to a . . ."

(A small gap.)

Column VI.

(Enkidu is speaking)

"Trouble I foresee wherever I go . . . .
O my friend, I have seen a dream which un- . . . ."
The day of the dream he had seen fulfilled . . . .

(Enkidu is stricken with fear at thought of the combat).

Enkidu lay for a day, yea, a second—for Enkidu lying
Prone on his couch, was a third and a fourth day . . ., a fifth, sixth and seventh,
Eighth, ninth, and tenth. While Enkidu lay in his sickness . . ., th' eleventh,
Aye, till the twelfth . . . on his couch was Enkidu lying.
Call'd he to Gilgamesh, ...
"O but, my comrade, . . . hateth me .. because within Uruk
I was afraid of the combat, and . . . My friend, who in battle . . ."

(A small gap in which Gilgamesh has answered. Enkidu replies):

Enkidu open'd his mouth and spake unto Gilgamesh, saying:
"Nay, but, my friend, let us no wise go down to the depths of the Forest,
For 'tis my hands have grown weak, and my arms are stricken with palsy."

Gilgamesh open'd his mouth and spake unto Enkidu, saying:
"Shall we, O friend, play the coward? . . . . . .
. . . . thou shalt surpass them all . . . .
Thou, O my friend, art cunning in warfare, art shrewd in the battle,
So shalt thou touch the . . . and of death have no terror,

(Two difficult and mutilated lines).

So that the palsy now striking thine arms may depart, and the weakness
Pass from thy hands! Be brave and resist! O my comrade, together
We will go down—let the combat in no wise diminish thy courage!
O forget death, and be fearful of nothing .. for he who is valiant,
Cautious and careful, by leading the way hath his own body guarded,
He 'tis will safeguard a comrade."
A name by their valour ..
They will establish. And now they together arrive at the barrier,
Still'd into silence their speech, and they themselves suddenly stopping.

The Fifth Tablet:
Of the Fight with Humbaba

Column I.

(The Wonders of the Forest).

Stood they and stared at the Forest, they gazed at the height of the Cedars,
Scanning the avenue into the Forest: and there where Humbaba
Stalk'd, was a path, and straight were his tracks, and good was the passage.
Eke they beheld the Mount of the Cedar, the home of th' Immortals,
Shrine of Irnini , the Cedar uplifting its pride 'gainst the mountain,
Fair was its shade, all full of delight, with bushes there spreading,
Spread, too, the . . . . the Cedar the incense . . . .

> *(After a few mutilated lines the Column breaks: the upper part of Column II contains
> about twenty lines badly mutilated; then the lower part is more complete, beginning with
> visions granted to the hero).*

Column II.

(Gilgamesh relates his dreams).

" Then came another dream to me, comrade, and this second vision
Pleasant, indeed, which I saw, for we twain were standing together
High on a peak of the mountains, and then did the mountain peak topple,
Leaving us twain to be like . . . which are born in the desert."
Enkidu spake to his comrade the dream to interpret, thus saying:
"Comrade, in sooth, this vision of thine unto us good fortune forbodeth,
Aye, 'tis a dream of great gain thou didst see, for, bethink you, O comrade,
Surely the mountain which thou hast beholden must needs be Humbaba.
Thus doth it mean we shall capture Humbaba, and throw down his carcase,
Leaving his corpse in abasement—to-morrow 's outcome will I shew thee".

Now at the fortieth league did they break their fast with a morsel,
Now at the sixtieth rested, and hollow'd a pit in the sunshine . . .
Gilgamesh mounted above it . . . and pour'd out his meal for the mountain:

"Mountain, a dream do thou grant . . . breathe on him . . ."

Column III.

Granted the mountain a dream . . . it breathed on him . . .
Then a chill wind-blast up-sprang and a gust passing over . . .
Made him to cower, and . . . thereat he sway'd like the corn of the mountains . . .
Gilgamesh, squatting bent-kneed, supported his haunches, and straightway
Sleep such as floweth on man descended upon him: at midnight
Ending his slumber all sudden, he hied him to speak to his comrade:
"Didst thou not call me, O friend? O, why am I waken'd from slumber?
Didst thou not touch me—for, why am I fearful, or hath not some spirit
Pass'd me? Or, why is my flesh all a-quiver?

(The dream of the volcano, which probably represents Humbaba).

A third dream, O comrade,

I have beheld: but all awesome this dream which I have beholden:
Loud did the firmament roar, and earth with the echo resounded,
Sombre the day, with darkness uprising, and levin bolts flashing,
Kindled were flames, and there, too, was Pestilence fill'd to o'erflowing,
Gorgéd was Death! Then faded the glare, then faded the fires,
Falling, the brands turn'd to ashes—Come, let us go down to the desert,
That we may counsel together."
Enkidu now to interpret his dream unto Gilgamesh speaketh:

(Remainder of Column III broken away).

A variant version is found on one of the Semitic tablets from Boghaz Keui .
Where the sense becomes connected it briefly describes how the heroes halt for
the night and at midnight sleep departs from the hero who tells his dream to En-
kidu, after asking much in the same way why he is frightened at waking from his
dream. "Besides my first dream a second . . . In my dream, O friend, a mountain . .
. he cast me down, seized my feet . . . The brilliance increased: a man . . ., most
comely of all the land was his beauty . . . Beneath the mountain he drew me, and . .
. water he gave me to drink, and my desire was assuaged; to earth he set my feet . .
. Enkidu unto this god . . . unto Gilgamesh spake: "My friend, we will go . . . what-
ever is hostile . . . Not the mountain . . . Come, lay aside fear . . . " The rest after
about mutilated seven lines is lost.

*(Column IV is all lost, and hardly anything of Column V remains. Column VI once
contained the story of the great fight, but except for a few broken lines at the end it is
all lost. But we can fortunately replace it from the Hittite version from Boghaz Keui)*

Column VI.

(The Fight with Humbaba).

In the following manner . . . the Sun-god in heaven . . . the trees:
He saw Gilgamesh: of the Sun-god in heaven in . . .
 And
shew'd him the dam on the ditches.
Gilgamesh spake then in orison unto the Sun-god in heaven;
"Lo, on that day to the city . . . . which is in the city:
I in sooth pray to the Sun-god in heaven: I on a road have now started,
. . . ."
Unto th' entreaty of Gilgamesh hearken'd the Sun-god in heaven,
Wherefore against Humbaba he raised mighty winds: yea, a great wind,
Wind from the North, aye, a wind from the South, yea a tempest and storm wind,
Chill wind, and whirlwind, a wind of all evil: 'twas eight winds he raiséd,
Seizing Humbaba before and behind, so that nor to go forwards,
Nor to go back was he able: and then Humbaba surrender'd.
Wherefore to Gilgamesh spake thus Humbaba: "O Gilgamesh, pr'y thee,
Stay, now, thy hand: be thou now my master, and I'll be thy henchman:
O disregard all the words which I spake so boastfull against thee,
Weighty . . . I would lay me down . . . and the Palace.
Thereat to Gilgamesh Enkidu spake: "Of the rede which Humbaba
Maketh to thee thou darest in nowise offer acceptance.
Aye, for Humbaba must not remain alive . . . ."

> *(The Hittite Version here breaks off. The Assyrian Version ends with six badly mutilated lines of which the last tells the successful issue of the expedition).*

. . . . they cut off the head of Humbaba.

The Sixth Tablet:
Of the Goddess Ishtar, Who Fell in Love with the Hero After His Exploit Against Humbaba

Column I.

(Gilgamesh is removing the stains of combat).

Now is he washing his stains, and is cleansing his garments in tatters,
Braiding the locks of his hair to descend loose over his shoulders,
Laying aside his garments besmirchen, and donning his clean ones,
Putting on armlets, and girding his body about with a baldric,
Gilgamesh bindeth his fillet, and girdeth himself with a baldric.

(Ishtar sees him and seeks to wed him).

Now Lady Ishtar espieth the beauty of Gilgamesh: saith she,
"Gilgamesh, come, be a bridegroom, to me of the fruit of thy body
Grant me largesse: for my husband shalt be and I'll be thy consort.
O, but I'll furnish a chariot for thee, all azure and golden,
Golden its wheel, and its yoke precious stones , each day to be harness'd
Unto great mules: O, enter our house with the fragrance of cedar.
So when thou enterest into our house shall threshold and dais
Kiss thy feet, and beneath thee do homage kings, princes, and rulers,
Bringing thee yield of the mountains and plains as a tribute: thy she-goats
Bring forth in plenty, thy ewes shall bear twins, thy asses attaining
Each to the size of a mule, and thy steeds in thy chariot winning
Fame for their gallop: thy mules in the yoke shall ne'er have a rival."

Gilgamesh open'd his mouth in reply, Lady Ishtar to answer:
"Aye, but what must I give thee, if I should take thee in marriage?
I must provide thee with oil for thy body, and clothing: aye, also
Give thee thy bread and thy victual: sooth, must be sustenance ample
Meet for divinity—I, too, must give thee thy drink fit for royalty.
. . . . I shall be bound, . . . let us amass, . . . clothe with a garment.

What, then, will be my advantage, supposing I take thee in marriage?
Thou'rt but a ruin which giveth no shelter to man from the weather,
Thou'rt but a back door not giving resistance to blast or to windstorm,

Thou'rt but a palace which dasheth the heroes within it to pieces,
Thou'rt but a pitfall which letteth its covering give way all treach'rous,
Thou art but pitch which defileth the man who doth carry it with him,
Thou'rt but a bottle which leaketh on him who doth carry it with him,
Thou art but limestone which letteth stone ramparts fall crumbling in ruin.
Thou'rt but chalcedony failing to guard in an enemy's country,
Thou'rt but a sandal which causeth its owner to trip by the wayside.
Who was ever thy husband thou faithfully lovedst for all time?
Who hath been ever thy lord who hath gain'd over thee the advantage?
Come, and I will unfold thee the endless tale of thy husbands.

Sooth, thou shalt vouch for the truth of this list—Thy maidenhood's consort,
Tammuz, each year dost make him the cause of Wailing , then cometh
Next the bird Roller gay-feather'd thou lovedst, and yet thou didst smite him
Breaking his wing: in the grove doth he stand, crying *kappi* 'my wing!'
Lovedst thou also a Lion, in all the full strength of his vigour,
Yet thou didst dig for him seven and seven deep pits to entrap him.
Lovedst thou also a Stallion, magnificent he in the battle,
Thou wert the cause of a bridle, a spur, and a whip to him: also
Thou wert the cause of his fifty miles galloping; thou wert the cause, too,
Eke, of exhaustion and sweating ; thereafter, 'twas thou who didst also
Unto his mother Silili give cause for her deep lamentation.
Lovedst thou also a Shepherd, a neatherd, for thee without ceasing
Each day to sacrifice yeanlings for thee would heap thee his charcoal,
Yet thou didst smite him, transforming him into a jackal: his herd boy
Yea, his own herd boy drove him away, and his dogs tore his buttocks.
Lovedst thou, too, Ishullanu, the gardener he of thy sire,
Bringing delights to thee ceaseless, while daily he garnish'd thy platter;
'Twas for thee only to cast thine eyes on him, and with him be smitten .
'O Ishullanu of mine, come, let me taste of thy vigour,
Put forth thy hand, too, ...
'

  But he, Ishullanu,

Said to thee 'What dost thou ask me? Save only my mother hath baked it,
Nought have I eaten—and what I should eat would be bread of transgression,
Aye and iniquity! Further, the reeds are a cloak against winter. '
Thou this his answer didst hear, didst smite him and make him a spider ,
Making him lodge midway up a dwelling —not to move upwards
Lest there be drainage ; nor down, lest a crushing o'erwhelm him.

So, too, me in my turn thou wouldst love and then reckon me like them."

Heard this then Ishtar: she burst into rage and went up to Heaven,
Hied her thus Ishtar to Anu, her father, to Antu, her mother,
Came she to tell them: "O father, doth Gilgamesh load me with insult,
Gilgamesh tale of my sins, my sins and iniquities telleth."

Anu made answer, thus speaking, and said unto Ishtar the Lady:
"Nay, thou didst ask him to grant thee largesse of the fruit of his body,
Hence he the tale of thy sins, thy sins and iniquities telleth."

(The Creation of the Divine Bull which is to destroy the heroes).

Ishtar made answer thus speaking, and said unto Anu, her father:
"Father, O make me a Heavenly Bull, which shall Gilgamesh vanquish,
Filling its body with flame . . . .
But if thou'lt not make this Bull, then . . . .
I'll smite . . . ., I'll put . . . ., I'll . . . .
More than the . . . will be the . . . .

Anu made answer, thus speaking, and said unto Ishtar, the Lady:
"If I the Heavenly Bull shall create, for which thou dost ask me,
Then seven years of leer husks must needs follow after his onslaught .
Wilt thou for man gather corn, and increase for the cattle the fodder ."

Ishtar made answer, thus speaking and said unto Anu, her father:
"Corn for mankind have I hoarded, have grown for the cattle the fodder,
If seven years of leer husks must needs follow after his onslaught
I will for man gather corn and increase for the cattle the fodder."

(Perhaps a small gap.)

About seven lines are so badly mutilated that little can be gleaned from them except that the fight with the Heavenly Bull is about to take place in Uruk. After these a hundred men descend upon the Bull, but with his fiery breath he annihilates them. Then come two hundred with the same result, and then three hundred more, again to be overcome.

Enkidu girded his middle; and straightway Enkidu, leaping,
Seized on the Heavenly Bull by his horns, and headlong before him
Cast down the Heavenly Bull his full length, ...
Aye, by the thick of his tail.

(Gap of thirteen mutilated lines.)

Chased him did Enkidu, . . . the Heavenly Bull . . .
Seized him and by the thick of his tail . . . .

Gap of about fourteen mutilated lines in which the Bull is slain.

So, what time they the Bull of the Heavens had kill'd, its heart they removéd,
Unto the Sun-god they offer'd in sacrifice; when the libation
Unto the Sun they had voided, they sate them down, the two brothers.

(The Frenzy of Ishtar).

Then mounted Ishtar the crest of the ramparts of Uruk, the high-wall'd,
So to the roof-top ascended, and there gave voice to her wailing;
"Woe unto Gilgamesh—he who by killing the Bull of the Heavens,
Made me lament." When Enkidu heard this, the shrieking of Ishtar,
Wrenching the member from out of the Bull, he toss'd it before her;
"If I could only have reach'd thee, i'faith, I'd ha' served thee the same way,
I'd ha' let dangle his guts on thy flanks as a girdle about thee."
Ishtar assembled the girl-devotees, the hetaerae and harlots,
Over the member torn out from the Bull she led the lamenting.

(The Triumph of Gilgamesh).

Gilgamesh call'd to the masters of craft, the artists, yea, all of them,
That at the size of its horns all the guilds of the crafts speak their praises
Each had of azure in weight thirty minas to be as their setting,
Two fingers their . ...
Both of them held six measures of oil; to his god Lugal-banda
He for his unguent devoting, brought in, and thus let them hang there,
There in the shrine of his forbears.
 And now in the River Euphrates
Washing their hands, they start on their progress and come to the city;
Now are they striding the highway of Uruk, the heroes of Uruk
Thronging about them to see them. Then Gilgamesh utter'd a riddle
Unto the notables :

Who, pr'ythee, is most splendid of heroes,
Who, pr'ythee, is most famous of giants?
Gilgamesh—he is most splendid of heroes,
Enkidu—he is most famous of giants.

(Three mutilated lines follow.)

So in his palace did Gilgamesh hold high revel: thereafter,
While all the heroes asleep, on their nightly couches were lying
Enkidu, too, was asleep, and a vision beheld, and so coming
Enkidu now his dream to reveal: thus spake he unto his comrade.

The Seventh Tablet:
The Death of Enkidu

Column I.

(Enkidu's dream).

"Why, O my friend, do the great gods now take counsel together?"

(The remainder of the Column is lost in the Assyrian, but it can be partially supplied from the Hittite Version: "... Then came the day ... [Enkidu] answered Gilgamesh: '[Gilgamesh, hear the] dream which I [saw] in the night: [Now Enlil], Ea, and the Sun-god of heaven ....[the Sun-god (?)] Enlil spake in return: "[These who the heavenly] Bull have kill'd [and Humbaba have smitten]:. . . which help'd at the cedar . . .[Enlil hath said (?)] 'Enkidu shall die: [but Gilgamesh] shall not die.'" Then answer'd Enlil boldly '[O Sun-god], at thy behest did they slay the Heavenly Bull and Humbaba. But now shall Enkidu die.' But Enlil turn'd angrily to the Sun-god: 'What dost thou them as befitting . . .? With his comrade thou settest out daily. "'But Enkidu laid himself down to rest before Gilgamesh, and by the dam . . . him the ditch: 'My brother, of (great) worth is my [dream].'" It breaks off after a few mutilated lines more).

Column II entirely lost. From the Hittite it is clear that Enkidu has dreamt that the gods have taken counsel together, that Enkidu is to die, but Gilgamesh remain alive. It would appear from the succeeding material that Enkidu, stricken presumably by fever, attributes all his misfortunes to the hetaera whom he loads with curses. The first part of the next fragment begins "destroy his power, weaken his strength," probably referring to Enkidu. Then says Enkidu, after three broken lines: ". . . . the hetaera . . . . who has brought a curse, 'O hetaera, I will decree thy fate for thee—thy woes . . . shall never end for all eternity. Come, I will curse thee with a bitter curse, . . . with desolation shall its curse come on thee: may there never be satisfaction of thy desire' —and then follow the broken ends of six lines and then—"'May . . . fall on thy house, may the . . of the street be thy dwelling, may the shade of the wall be thy abode, . . . for thy feet, may scorching heat and thirsty smite thy strength'" The rest of the curse is badly broken, but it is exceeding probable that the following are the fragments which should be assigned here.

(The End of Enkidu's curse on the Hetaera).

"Of want . . . . since me it is that . . .hath . . . .
And me the fever hath laid on my back."

(The Answer of Shamash).

Heard him the Sun-god, and open'd his mouth, and from out of the heavens
Straightway he call'd him: "O Enkidu, why dost thou curse the hetaera?

She 'twas who made thee eat bread, for divinity proper: aye, wine too,
She made thee drink, 'twas for royalty proper: a generous mantle
Put on thee, aye, and for comrade did give to thee Gilgamesh splendid.
Now on a couch of great size will he, thy friend and thy brother
Gilgamesh, grant thee to lie, on a handsome couch will he grant thee
Rest, and to sit on a throne of great ease, a throne at his left hand,
So that the princes of Hades may kiss thy feet in their homage;
He, too, will make all the people of Uruk lament in thy honour,
Making them mourn thee, and damsels and heroes constrain to thy service,
While he himself for thy sake will cause his body to carry
Stains, and will put on the skin of a lion , and range o'er the desert."

Enkidu then giving ear to the words of the valiant Shamash
Speaking . . . . his wrath was appeased.

(One or two lines missing).

Column IV.

(Enkidu, relenting, regrets his curse, and blesses the Hetaera).

" . . . . may . . . restore to thy place!
So, too, may monarchs and princes and chiefs be with love for thee smitten;
None smite his breech in disgust ; against thee; and for thee may the hero
Comb out his locks; . . . who would embrace thee,
Let him his girdle unloose . . . and thy bed be azure and golden;
May . . . entreat thee kindly, ... are heap'd his *ishshikku*
May the gods make thee enter . . . .
Mayst thou be left as the mother of seven brides . . ."

(Enkidu, sorrowful at his approaching end, sleeps alone and dreams).

Enkidu . . . woe in his belly . . . sleeping alone,
Came in the night to discover his heaviness unto his comrade:
"Friend, O a dream I have seen in my night-time: the firmament roaring,
Echo'd the earth, and I by myself was standing . . .
When perceived I a man, all dark was his face, and was liken 'd
Unto . . .his face, . . . and his nails like claws of a lion.
20.Me did he overcome . . . climbing up . . . press'd me down,

Upon me . . . my body . . . . . .

> *(Here follows a gap of perhaps three lines, until what is still presumably the dream is
> again taken up by the other half of the Column at l. 31 (?) with a description of the
> Underworld which is being shewn to Enkidu in premonition of his death).*

. . . . like birds my hands: and he seized me,
Me did he lead to the Dwelling of Darkness, the home of Irkalla,
35.Unto the Dwelling from which he who entereth cometh forth never!
Aye, by the road on the passage whereof there can be no returning,
Unto the Dwelling whose tenants are ever bereft of the daylight,
Where for their food is the dust, and the mud is their sustenance: bird-like
Wear they a garment of feathers: and, sitting there in the darkness,
Never the light will they see. On the Gate . . . . when I enter'd
On the house . . . . was humbled the crown,
For . . . those who wore crowns, who of old ruled over the country,
. . . . of Anu and Enlil 'twas they set the bakemeats,
Set . . . ., cool was the water they served from the skins. When I enter'd
Into this House of the Dust, were High Priest and acolyte sitting,
Seer and magician , the priest who the Sea of the great gods anointed ,
Here sat Etana , Sumuqan; the Queen of the Underworld also,
Ereshkigal , in whose presence doth bow the Recorder of Hades,
Belit-seri, and readeth before her; she lifted her head and beheld me,
. . . and took this . . . .

> *(The text here breaks off).*

The Eighth Tablet:
Of the Mourning of Gilgamesh, and What Came of It

(The first Column is badly mutilated, and all we can glean from it is that "as soon as something of morning has dawned," Gilgamesh addressing Enkidu, compares him to a gazelle, and promises to glorify him. Then follows apparently a recital by Gilgamesh of their exploits together, "mountains [we ascended, we reach'd] the Forest of Cedars, [travelling] night and day . . . [with wild beasts (?)] drawing nigh after us." Enkidu is lying dying or dead, and Column II begins with Gilgamesh keening over his dead friend before the Elders of Uruk):

"Unto me hearken, O Elders, to me, aye, me shall ye listen,
'Tis that I weep for my comrade Enkidu, bitterly crying
Like to a wailing woman: my grip is slack'd on the curtleaxe
Slung at my thigh, and the brand at my belt from my sight is removed.
Aye, and my festal attire lends nought of its aid for my pleasure,
Me, me hath sorrow assailed, and cast me down in affliction.

Comrade and henchman, who chased the wild ass , the pard of the desert,
Comrade and henchman, who chased the wild ass , the pard of the desert,
Enkidu—we who all haps overcame, ascending the mountains.
Captured the Heavenly Bull, and destroy'd him: we o'erthrew Humbaba,
He who abode in the Forest of Cedars —O, what is this slumber
Now hath o'ercome thee, for now art thou dark, nor art able to hear me?"
 Natheless he raised not his eyes, and his heart, when
Gilgamesh felt it,
Made no beat.
 Then he
veil'd his friend like a bride ..
Lifted his voice like a lion . . . .
Roar'd like a lioness robb'd of her whelps. In front of his comrade
Paced he backwards and forwards, tearing and casting his ringlets,
Plucking and casting away all the grace of his . . . .

Then when something of morning had dawn'd, did Gilgamesh . . . .

(Column II here breaks off. Column III begins with Gilgamesh still mourning, telling his dead friend all he will do for him in the words of Shamash in the preceding tablet, so that we may supply the last two (?) lines of Column II as follow):

Column II.

(The Lament of Gilgamesh).

"O, on a couch of great size will I, thy friend and thy brother,

Column III.

Gilgamesh, grant thee to lie, on a handsome couch will I grant thee
Rest, and to sit on a throne of great size, a throne at my left hand,
So that the princes of Hades may kiss thy feet in their homage;
I, too, will make all the people of Uruk lament in thy honour,
Making them mourn thee, and damselsandheroesconstrain to thy service,
While I myself for thy sake will cause my body to carry
Stains, and will put on the skin of a lion , and range o'er the desert."

Then when something of morning had dawn'd did Gilgamesh . . . .
Loosing his girdle . . . .

(Column IV has only five fragmentary lines at the end, mentioning "to my friend," "thy sword," "likeness," and "to the god Bibbu," i.e., a planet or Mercury. Column V has only a bare dozen fragmentary lines at the end):

Column V.

" . . . Judge of the Anunnaki . . ."

Then, when Gilgamesh heard this, he form'd of the slaying a concept .

Then, with the dawn of the morning did Gilgamesh fashion a . . .
Brought out also a mighty platter of wood from the highlands .
Fill'd he with honey a bowl of bright ruby , a bowl too of azure,
Fill'd he with cream; and adorn'd he the . . ., and Shamash instructed ..

(One line lost at end of Column. Column VI is all lost).

The Ninth Tablet: Gilgamesh in Terror of Death Seeks Eternal Life

Column I.

(Gilgamesh determines to seek Eternal Life).

Gilgamesh bitterly wept for his comrade, for Enkidu, ranging
Over the desert: "I, too—shall I not die like Enkidu also?
Sorrow hath enter'd my heart; I fear death as I range o'er the desert,
I will get hence on the road to the presence of Uta-Napishtim , —Offspring of
Ubara-Tutu is he—and with speed will I travel.
If 'tis in darkness that I shall arrive at the Gates of the Mountains,
Meeting with lions, then terror fall on me, I'll lift my head skywards,
Offer my prayer to the Moon-god, or else to . . the gods let my orison
Come . . . 'O deliver me!'" . . . He slept . . . and a dream . . .
Saw he . . . which were rejoicing in life,
Poised he his axe . . . in his hand, and drew his glaive from his baldric,
Lance-like leapt he amongst them . . . smiting, . . . and crushing.

(The rest of the Column is mutilated).

Column II.
(The hero reaches the Mountains of Mashu).

Mashu the name of the hills; as he reach'd the Mountains of Mashu,
Where ev'ry day they keep watch o'er the Sun-god's rising and setting,
Unto the Zenith of Heaven uprear'd are their summits, and downwards
Deep unto Hell reach their breasts: and there at their portals stand sentry
Scorpion-men, awful in terror, their very glance Death: and tremendous,
Shaking the hills, their magnificence; they are the Wardens of Shamash,
Both at his rising and setting. No sooner did Gilgamesh see them"
Than from alarm and dismay was his countenance stricken with pallor,
Senseless, he grovell'd before them.
 Then unto his wife spake the Scorpion:

"Lo, he that cometh to us—'tis the flesh of the gods is his body."
Then to the Scorpion-man answerd his wife: "Two parts of him god-like,

Only a third of him human."

> *(Eight broken lines remain, in which the Scorpion-man addresses presumably Gilga-mesh, asking him [why he has goner a far journey, and telling him how hard the traverse is. Column III begins with the third line in which Gilgamesh is evidently tell-ing the Scorpion-man that he proposes to cask(?)] Uta-Napishtim about death and life. But the Scorpion-man says that [the journey has never before been made, that none [has crossed] the mountains. The traverse is by the Road of the Sun by a journey of twenty-four hours, beginning with deep darkness. The last half of this Column and the first half of Column IV are lost, but it would appear that the Scorpion-man describes the journey hour by hour, and that Gilgamesh accepts the trial of his strength "[even though it be] in pain . ., [though my face be weather]d] with cold [and heat] (and) in grief [I go] . . ." Then the Scorpion-man, with a final word about the mountains of Mashu, farewells him, wishing him success. "[(Then) when] Gilgamesh [heard this], [he set off] at the word of the Scorpion-man, taking] the Road of the Sun . . ." The first two hours are in deep darkness, without light, which did not allow [him to see . . . behind him] . . .*

" Each succeeding period of two hours is the same until the eighth is reached and passed, and by the ninth he apparently comes to the first glimmer of light. Finally, with the twelfth double hour, he reaches the full blaze of the sun, and there he be-holds the Tree of the Gods, the description of which is given in the only four complete lines,48-51, of Column V. It is conceivable that this is the Vine, the Tree of Life, whence Siduri, the Maker of Wine, plucks the fruit for her trade.

Bearing its fruit all ruby, and hung about with its tendrils.
Fair for beholding, and azure the boskage it bore; aye, 'twas bearing
Fruits all desirable unto the eye.

> *(Column VI in the Assyrian is nearly all lost, and it is uncertain what part the Tree plays: but at this point a third Old Babylonian tablet helps us out. At this point, ac-cording to this early version the Sun-god takes pity on the hero).*

"He of the wild things hath dresséd their pelts and the flesh of them eateth.
Gilgamesh, never a crossing shall be where none hath been ever,
No, so long as the gale driveth water."
Shamash was touch'd, that he summon'd him, thus unto Gilgamesh speaking:
"Gilgamesh, why dost thou run, forasmuch as the life which thou seekest
Thou shalt not find?" Whereat Gilgamesh answer'd the warrior Shamash:
"Shall I, after I roam up and down o'er the waste as a wand'rer,
Lay my head in the bowels of earth, and throughout the years slumber
Ever and aye? Let mine eyes see the Sun and be sated with brightness,
Yea, for the darkness is banish'd afar, if wide be the brightness.
When will the man who is dead ever look on the light of the Sunshine?"

With this ends all our connected text of Column VI, the Assyrian Version ending with about a dozen mutilated lines containing a mention of numerous minerals and stones, and evidently Gilgamesh has now come to the girl Siduri the sabitu, which last word is generally taken to mean a provider of strong waters.

The Tenth Tablet: How Gilgamesh Reached Uta-Napishtim

Column I.

Gilgamesh meets Siduri.

Dwelt Siduri, the maker of wine . . . .
Wine was her trade, her trade was . . . .
Cover'd she was with a veil and . . . .
Gilgamesh wander'd towards her . . . .
Pelts was he wearing . . . .
Flesh of the gods in his body possessing, but woe in his belly,
Aye, and his countenance like to a man who hath gone a far journey.
Look'd in the distance the maker of wine, and a word in her bosom
Quoth she, in thought with herself: "This is one who would ravish a woman,
Whither doth he advance in . . . ?" As soon as the Wine-maker saw him,
Barr'd she her postern, barr'd she her inner door, barr'd she her chamber.
Straightway did Gilgamesh, too, in his turn catch the sound of her shutting,
Lifted his chin, and so did he let his attention fall on her.

Unto her therefore did Gilgamesh speak, to the Wine-maker saying:
"Wine-maker, what didst thou see, that thy postern now thou hast barréd,
Barréd thine inner door, -barréd thy chamber? O, I'll smite thy portal,
Breaking the bolt . . . .

About nine lines mutilated, after which it is possible to restore l. 32—Column II, 8.

Unto him answer'd the Wine-maker, speaking to Gilgamesh, saying:
"Why is thy vigour so wasted, or why is thy countenance sunken,
Why hath thy spirit a sorrow, or why hath thy cheerfulness surcease?
O, but there's woe in thy belly! Like one who hath gone a far journey
So is thy face—O, with cold and with heat is thy countenance weather'd,
. . . that thou shouldst range over the desert."
Gilgamesh unto her answer'd and spake to the Wine-maker, saying:
"Wine-maker, 'tis not my vigour is wasted, nor countenance sunken,

Nor hath my spirit a sorrow, forsooth, nor my cheerfulness surcease,

No, 'tis not woe in my belly: nor doth my visage resemble
One who hath gone a far journey—nor is my countenance weather'd
Either by cold or by heat . . . that thus I range over the desert.
Comrade and henchman, who chased the wild ass, the pard of the desert,
Comrade and henchman, who chased the wild ass, the pard of the desert,
Enkidu—we who all haps overcame, ascending the mountains,
Captured the Heavenly Bull, and destroy'd him: we o'erthrew Humbaba,
He who abode in the Forest of Cedars; we slaughter'd the lions

Column II.

There in the Gates of the mountains ; with me enduring all hardships,
Enkidu, he was my comrade—the lions we slaughter'd together,
Aye, enduring all hardships—and him his fate hath o'ertaken.
So did I mourn him six days, yea, a se'nnight, until unto burial
I could consign him . . . . then did I fear . . . . .
Death did I dread, that I range o'er the desert: the hap of my comrade
Lay on me heavy—O 'tis a long road that I range o'er the desert!
Enkidu, yea, of my comrade the hap lay heavy upon me—
'Tis a long road that I range o'er the desert—O, how to be silent,
Aye, or how to give voice? For the comrade I ha' so lovéd
Like to the dust hath become; O Enkidu, he was my comrade,
He whom I loved hath become alike the dust—I, shall I not, also,
Lay me down like him, throughout all eternity never returning?"

> *(Here may be interpolated, for convenience, the Old Babylonian Version of this episode in the Berlin tablet of 2000B.C. Column II, 1,-III, 14):*

Column II.

"He who enduréd all hardships with me, whom I lovéd dearly,
Enkidu,—he who enduréd all hardships with me is now perish'd,
Gone to the common lot of mankind! And I have bewail'd him
Day and night long: and unto the tomb I have not consign'd him.
O but my friend cometh not to my call—six days, yea, a se'nnight
He like a worm hath lain on his face—and I for this reason
Find no life, but must needs roam the desert like to a hunter,
Wherefore, O Wine-maker, now that at last I look on thy visage,
Death which I dread I will see not!"

> *(The Philosophy of the Wine-maker).*

The Wine-maker
Gilgamesh answer'd:

Column III.

"Gilgamesh, why runnest thou, inasmuch as the life which thou seekest,
Thou canst not find? For the gods, in their first creation of mortals,
Death allotted to man, but life they retain'd in their keeping.
Gilgamesh, full be thy belly,
Each day and night be thou merry, and daily keep holiday revel,
Each day and night do thou dance and rejoice; and fresh be thy raiment,
Aye, let thy head be clean washen, and bathe thyself in the water,
Cherish the little one holding thy hand; be thy spouse in thy bosom
Happy—for this is the dower of man . . . . .

(Here the Old Babylonian Version breaks off and we must return to the Assyrian).

(Gilgamesh, dissatisfied with a Wine-maker's philosophy, would seek further afield).

Gilgamesh thus continued his speech to the Wine-maker, saying,
"Pr'ythee, then, Wine-maker, which is the way unto Uta-Napishtim?
What is its token, I pr'ythee, vouchsafe me, vouchsafe me its token.
If it be possible even the Ocean itself will I traverse,
But if it should be impossible, then will I range o'er the desert."

(The Wine-maker, in accordance with tradition, attempts to dissuade him).

Thus did the Wine-maker answer to him, unto Gilgamesh saying,
"There hath been never a crossing, O Gilgamesh: never aforetime
Anyone, coming thus far, hath been able to traverse the Ocean:
Warrior Shamash doth cross it , 'tis true, but who besides Shamash
Maketh the traverse? Yea, rough is the ferry, and rougher its passage,
Aye, too, 'tis deep are the Waters of Death, which bar its approaches .
Gilgamesh, if perchance thou succeed in traversing the Ocean,
What wilt thou do, when unto the Waters of Death thou arrivest?
Gilgamesh, there is Ur-Shanabi, boatman to Uta-Napishtim,
He with whom sails are, the *urnu* of which in the forest he plucketh,
Now let him look on thy presence, and if it be possible with him
Cross—but if it be not, then do thou retrace thy steps homewards."

Gilgamesh, hearing this, taketh his axe in his hand, awhile he draweth Glaive from
his baldric .

*(The remainder of this Column in the Assyrian Version is so much mutilated that lit-
tle can be made out, but what is obviously essential is that Gilgamesh meets Ur-
Shanabi, but destroys the sails (?) of the boat for some reason. Before going on with the
restoration of the Assyrian Version, we can interpolate Column IV from the Old
Babylonian Version of the Berlin Tablet)*

Then did Ur-Shanabi speak to him yea, unto Gilgamesh, saying:
"Tell to me what is thy name, for I am Ur-Shanabi, henchman,
Aye, of far Uta-Napishtim ." To him did Gilgamesh answer:

"Gilgamesh, that is my name, come hither from Uruk, E-Anni,
One who hath traversed the Mountains, a wearisome journey of Sunrise,
Now that I look on thy face, Ur-Shanabi—Uta-Napishtim
Let me see also—the Distant one!" Him did Ur-Shanabi answer,
Gilgamesh: . . . ."

*(In the Assyrian Version Ur-Shanabi presently addresses Gilgamesh in exactly the
same words as Siduri, the Wine-maker, with the same astonishment at his weather-
beaten appearance):*

Column III.

Thus did Ur-Shanabi speak to him, yea, unto Gilgamesh, saying
"Why is thy vigour all wasted . . ."

*(It continues thus, to be supplied for ll. 2-31 from Columns I, 33-II, 14 with due
bracketing for the last words, and then the text goes on):*

Gilgamesh thus continued his speech to Ur-Shanabi, saying
"Pr'ythee, Ur-Shanabi, which is the way unto Uta-Napishtim ?
What is its token, I pr'ythee, vouchsafe me, vouchsafe me nits token.
If it be possible even the Ocean itself will I traverse,
But if it should be impossible, then will I range o'er the desert."

Thus did Ur-Shanabi speak to him, yea, unto Gilgamesh, saying:
"Gilgamesh, 'tis thine own hand hath hinder'd thy crossing the Ocean,
Thou hast destroyéd the sails, and hast piercéd the . . .
Now destroy'd are the sails, and the *urnu* not . . . . .

Gilgamesh, take thee thy axe in thy hand; O, descend to the forest,
Fashion thee poles each of five gar in length; make knops of bitumen,
Sockets, too, add to them : bring them me." Thereat, when Gilgamesh heard this,
Took he the axe in his hand, and the glaive drew forth from his baldric,
Went to the forest, and poles each of five gar in length did he fashion,
Knops of bitumen he made, and he added their sockets: and brought them . . ,
Gilgamesh then, and Ur-Shanabi fared them forth in their vessel,
Launch'd they the boat on the billow, and they themselves in her embarking.
After the course of a month and a half he saw on the third day
How that Ur-Shanabi now at the Waters of Death had arrivéd.

Column IV.

Thus did Ur-Shanabi answer him, yea, unto Gilgamesh, saying:
"Gilgamesh, take the . . . . away . . . .
Let not the Waters of Death touch thy hand . . . . . .
Gilgamesh, take thou a second, a third, and a fourth pole for thrusting,
Gilgamesh, take thou a fifth, and a sixth, and a seventh for thrusting,
Gilgamesh, take thou an eighth, and a ninth, and a tenth pole for thrusting,

Gilgamesh, take an eleventh, a twelfth pole!" He ceased from his poling,
Aye with twice-sixty thrusts; then ungirded his loins . . . .
Gilgamesh . . . ., and set up the mast in its socket.

He reaches Uta-Napishtim.

Uta-Napishtim look'd into the distance and, inwardly musing,
Said to himself: "Now, why are the sails of the vessel destroyéd,
Aye, and one who is not of my . . . doth ride on the vessel?
This is no mortal who cometh: nor . . . .
I look, but this is no mortal . . . . . .
I look, but . . . . . I look but . . . . .

> *(Remainder of Column lost, but about l. 42 it becomes apparent that Uta-Napishtim is asking Gilgamesh in exactly the same words as Siduri, the Wine-maker, and Ur-Shanabi "Why is thy vigour (all) wasted?" and so on, down to Column V, l. 22 "[I], shall I not also lay me down like him, throughout all eternity never returning?"):*

Gilgamesh thus continued his speech unto Uta-Napishtim,
"Then I bethought me, I'll get hence and see what far Uta-Napishtim

Saith on the matter . And so, again I came through all countries,
Travell'd o'er difficult mountains, aye, and all seas have I traversed,
Nor hath ever my face had its fill of gentle sleep : but with hardship
Have I exhausted myself, and my flesh have I laden with sorrow.
Ere I had come to the House of the Wine-Maker, spent were my garments,
. . . Owl, bat, lion, pard, wild cat, deer, ibex, and . . . . . .
Flesh of them all have I eaten, and eke their pelts have I dress'd me."

> *(The remainder of the Column is mutilated: there is some mention of "let them bolt her gate . . .; with pitch and bitumen . . . ." in l. 33, and then nothing which gives connected sense until Column VI, ll. 26-39):*

Column VI.

"Shall we for ever build houses, for ever set signet to contract,
Brothers continue to share, or among foes always be hatred?
Or will for ever the stream that hath risen in spate bring a torrent,
Kulilu-bird to *Kirippu*-bird . . . . ?
Face which doth look on the sunlight . . . presently shall not be . . .
Sleeping and dead arer alike, from Death they mark no distinction
Servant and master, when once thy have reach'd their full span allotted,
Then do the Anunnaki, great gods, ...
Mammetum, Maker of Destiny with them, doth destiny settle,
Death, aye, and Life they determine; of Death is the day not revealéd."

The Eleventh Tablet: The Flood

Column I.

(The Cause of the Flood).

Gilgamesh unto him spake, to Uta-Napishtim the Distant:
"Uta-Napishtim, upon thee I gaze, yet in no wise thy presence
Strange is, for thou art like me, and in no wise different art thou;
Thou art like me; yea a stomach for fighting doth make thee consummate,
Aye, and to rest on thy back thou dost lie. O tell me, how couldst thou
Stand in th' Assemblage of Gods to petition for life everlasting?"

Uta-Napishtim addressing him thus unto Gilgamesh answer'd:
"Gilgamesh, I unto thee will discover the whole hidden story,
Aye, and the rede of the Gods will I tell thee.
The City Shurippak —
O 'tis a city thou knowest!—is set on the marge of Euphrates,
Old is this city, with gods in its midst. Now, the great gods a deluge
Purposed to bring: . . . . . . there was Anu, their sire; their adviser
Warrior Enlil; Ninurta , their herald; their leader Ennugi;
Nin-igi-azag—'tis Ea—, albeit conspirator with them,
Unto a reed-hut their counsel betray'd he: "O Reed-hut, O Reed-hut!
Wall, wall! Hearken, O Reed-hut, consider, O Wall! O thou Mortal,
Thou of Shurippak, thou scion of Ubara-Tutu, a dwelling
Pull down, and fashion a vessel therewith; abandon possessions,
Life do thou seek, and thy hoard disregard, and save life; every creature
Make to embark in the vessel. The vessel, which thou art to fashion,
Apt be its measure; its beam and its length be in due correspondence,
Then on the deep do thou launch it." And I—sooth, I apprehending,
This wise to Ea, my lord, did I speak: 'See, Lord, what thou sayest
Thus, do I honour, I'll do—but to city, to people, and elders
Am I, forsooth, to explain?' Then Ea made answer in speaking,
Saying to me—me, his henchman!—'Thou mortal, shalt speak to them this wise:
"'Tis me alone whom Enlil so hateth that I in your city
No more may dwell, nor turn my face unto the land which is Enlil's.

I will go down to the Deep, there dwelling with Ea, my liege lord,
Wherefore on you will he shower down plenty, yea, fowl in great number,
Booty of fish . . . . and big the harvest.
. . . . causing a plentiful rainfall to come down upon you."'

Then when something of morning had dawn'd . . . .

(Five lines mutilated).

Pitch did the children provide, while the strong brought all that was needful.
Then on the fifth day after I laid out the shape of my vessel,
Ten *gar* each was the height of her sides, in accord with her planning,
Ten *gar* to match was the size of her deck, and the shape of the forepart

Did I lay down, and the same did I fashion; aye, six times cross-pinn'd her,
Sevenfold did I divide her . . . ., divided her inwards
Ninefold: hammer'd the caulking within her, and found me a quant-pole,
All that was needful I added; the hull with six *shar* of bitumen
Smear'd I, and three *shar* of pitch did I smear on the inside; some people,
Bearing a vessel of grease, three *shar* of it brought me; and one *shar*
Out of this grease did I leave, which the tackling consumed; and the boatman
Two *shar* of grease stow'd away; yea, beeves for the . . . I slaughter'd,
Each day lambs did I slay: mead, beer, oil, wine, too, the workmen
Drank as though they were water , and made a great feast like the New Year,

(Five mutilated lines "I added salve for the hand(s)," "the vessel was finish'd . . . Sha-mash the great." "was difficult," ". . ? I caused to bring above and below," "two-thirds of it"):

All I possess'd I laded aboard her; the silver I laded
All I possess'd; gold, all I possess'd I laded aboard her,
All I possess'd of the seed of all living I laded aboard her.
Into the ship I embark'd all my kindred and family with me,
Cattle and beasts of the field and all handicraftsmen embarking.
Then decreed Shamash the hour: " . . . .
Shall in the night let a plentiful rainfall pour down . . . .
Then do thou enter the vessel, and straightway shut down thy hatchway."
 Came then that hour appointed, ...
Did in the night let a plentiful rainfall pour down . . . .
View'd I the aspect of day: to look on the day bore a horror,
Wherefore I enter'd the vessel, and straightway shut down my hatchway,
So, too to shut down the vessel to Puzur-Amurri, the boatman,
Did I deliver the poop of the ship, besides its equipment.

Then, when something of dawn had appear'd, from out the horizon
Rose a cloud darkling; lo, Adad the storm-god was rumbling within it,
Nabu and Sharru were leading the vanguard, and coming as heralds
Over the hills and the levels: then Irragal wrench'd out the bollards;

Havoc Ninurta let loose as he came, th' Anunnaki their torches
Brandish'd, and shrivell'd the land with their flames; desolation from Adad
Stretch'd to high Heaven, and all that was bright was turn'd into darkness.

> *(Four lines mutilated "the land like . . .," "for one day the st[orm] . . ., " "fiercely*
> *blew . . . . " "like a battle . . . ").*

Nor could a brother distinguish his brother; from heaven were mortals
Not to be spied. O, were stricken with terror the gods at the Deluge,
Fleeing, they rose to the Heaven of Anu, and crouch'd in the outskirts,
Cow 'ring like curs were the gods while like to a woman in travail
Ishtar did cry, she shrieking aloud, e'en the sweet-spoken Lady
She of the gods: 'May that day turn to dust, because I spake evil
There in th' Assemblage of Gods! O, how could I utter such evil
There in the Assemblage of Gods, so to blot out my people, ordaining
Havoc! Sooth, then, am I to give birth, unto these mine own people
Only to glut with their bodies the Sea as though they were fish-spawn?'
Gods—Anunnaki—wept with her, the gods were sitting all humbled,
Aye, in their weeping, and closed were their lips amidthe Assemblage.
Six days, a se'nnight the hurricane, deluge, and tempest continued
Sweeping the land: when the seventh day came, were quelléd the warfare,
Tempest and deluge which like to an army embattail'd were fighting.
Lull'd was the sea, all spent was the gale, assuaged was the deluge,
So did I look on the day; lo, sound was all still'd; and all human
Back to its clay was return'd, and fen was level with roof-tree.
Then I open'd a hatchway, and down on my cheek stream'd the sunlight,
Bowing myself, I sat weeping, my tears o'er my cheeks overflowing,
Into the distance I gazed, to the furthest bounds of the Ocean,
Land was uprear'd at twelve points, and the Ark on the Mountain of Nisir
Grounded; the Mountain of Nisir held fast, nor gave lease to her shifting.
One day, nay, two, did Nisir hold fast, nor give lease to her shifting.
Three days, nay, four, did Nisir hold fast, nor give lease to her shifting,
Five days, nay, six, did Nisir hold fast, nor give lease to her shifting.
Then, when the seventh day dawn'd, I put forth a dove, and released her,
But to and fro went the dove, and return'd for a resting-place was not.
Then I a swallow put forth and released; to and fro went the swallow,
She too return'd, for a resting-place was not; I put forth a raven,
Her, too, releasing; the raven went, too, and th' abating of waters
Saw; and she ate as she waded and splash'd, unto me not returning.
Unto the four winds of heaven I freed all the beasts, and an off'ring
Sacrificed, and a libation I pour'd on the peak of the mountain,
Twice seven flagons devoting, and sweet cane, and cedar, and myrtle,

Heap'd up beneath them; the gods smelt the savour, the gods the sweet savour
Smelt; aye, the gods did assemble like flies o'er him making the off'ring.

Then, on arriving, the Queen of the gods the magnificent jewels
Lifted on high, which Anu had made in accord with her wishes;
'O ye Gods! I will rather forget this my necklet of sapphires,
Than not maintain these days in remembrance, nor ever forget them.
So, though the rest of the gods may present themselves at the off'ring,
Enlil alone of the gods may himself not come to the off'ring,
Because he, unreasoning, brought on a deluge, and therefore my people
Unto destruction consign'd.'
Then Enlil, on his arrival,
Spied out the vessel, and straightway did Enlil burst into anger,
Swollen with wrath 'gainst the gods, the Igigi : 'Hath any of mortals
'Scaped? Sooth, never a man could have lived through the welter of ruin.'
Then did Ninurta make answer and speak unto warrior Enlil,
Saying: 'O, who can there be to devise such a plan, except Ea?
Surely, 'tis Ea is privy to ev'ry design.' Whereat Ea
Answer'd and spake unto Enlil, the warrior, saying: 'O chieftain
Thou of the gods, thou warrior! How, forsooth, how all uncounsell'd
Couldst thou a deluge bring on? Aye, visit his sin on the sinner
Visit his guilt on the guilty, but O, have mercy, that thereby
He shall not be cut off; be clement, that he may not perish.
O, instead of thy making a flood, let a lion come, man to diminish;
O, instead of thy making a flood, let a jackal come, man to diminish;
O, instead of thy making a flood, let a famine occur, that the country
May be devour'd; instead of thy making a flood, let the Plague-god
Come and the people o'erwhelm;
  Sooth, indeed
'twas not I of the Great Gods the secret revealéd,
But to th' Abounding in Wisdom vouchsafed I a dream, and in this wise
He of the gods heard the secret. Deliberate, now, on his counsel'.
Then to the Ark came up Enlil; my hand did he grasp, and uplifted
Me, even me, and my wife, too, he raised, and, bent-kneed beside me,
Made her to kneel; our foreheads he touch'd as he stood there between us,
Blessing us; 'Uta-Napishtim hath hitherto only been mortal,
Now, indeed, Uta-Napishtim and also his wife shall be equal
Like to us gods; in the distance afar at the mouth of the rivers
Uta-Napishtim shall dwell'. So they took me and there in the distance

Caused me to dwell at the mouth of the rivers.
But thee, as for thee, pray,
Who will assemble the gods for thy need, that the life which thou seekest
Thou mayst discover? Come, fall not asleep for six days, aye, a se'nnight!"

   (But Gilgamesh is too mortal to resist even sleep).

Then, while he sat on his haunches a sleep like a breeze breathed upon him.
Spake to her, Uta-Napishtim, yea, unto his wife: "O, behold him,

E'en the strong fellow who asketh for life, how hath breathéd upon him
Sleep like a breeze!" Then his wife unto Uta-Napishtim the Distant
Answer'd: "O, touch him, and let the man wake, that the road he hath traversed
He may betake himself homeward in peace, that he by the portal
Whence he fared forth may return to his land." Spake Uta-Napishtim,
Yea, to his wife: "How the troubles of mortals do trouble thee also!
Bake then his flour and put at his head, but the time he is sleeping
On the house-wall do thou mark it. " So straightway she did so, his flour
Baked she and set at his head, but the time he was sleeping she noted
On the house-wall. So, *first* was collected his flour, then *secondly* sifted,
Thirdly, 'twas moisten'd, and *fourthly* she kneaded his dough, and so *fifthly*
Leaven she added, and sixthly 'twas baked; then *seventh*—he touch'd him,
All on a sudden, and so from his slumber awoke the great fellow!

Gilgamesh unto him spake, yea to Uta-Napishtim the Distant:
"Tell me, I pr'ythee, was 't thou, who when sleep was shower'd upon me
All on a sudden didst touch me, and straightway rouse me from slumber?"
Uta-Napishtim to Gilgamesh spake, yea, unto him spake he:
"Gilgamesh, told was the tale of thy meal . . . and then did I wake thee:
'One'—was collected thy flour: then *'two'*—it was sifted; and *'thirdly'*—
Moisten'd: and *'fourthly'*—she kneaded thy dough and *'fifthly'* the leaven
Added: and *'sixthly'*—'twas baked: and *'seventh'*—'twas I on a sudden
Touch'd thee and thou didst awake." To Uta-Napishtim, the Distant,
230.Gilgamesh answer'd: "O, how shall I act, or where shall I hie me,
Uta-Napishtim? A Robber from me hath ravish'd my courage,
Death in my bed-chamber broodeth, and Death is wherever I listen ."

Spake to him, yea, to the boatman Ur-Shanabi Uta-Napishtim:

"'Tis thou, Ur-Shanabi . . . the crossing, will hate thee,
Sooth, to all those who come to its marge, doth its marge set a limit:
This man for whom thou wert guide—are stains to cover his body,
Or shall a skin hide the grace of his limbs? Ur-Shanabi, take him,
Lead him to where he may bathe, that he wash off his stains in the water
White as the snow: let him cast off his pelts that the sea may remove them;
Fair let his body appear: of his head be the fillet renewéd,
Let him, as clothes for his nakedness, garb himself in a mantle,
Such that, or ever he come to his city, and finish his journey,
No sign of age shall the mantle betray, but preserve all its freshness."
Wherefore Ur-Shanabi took him, and where he might bathe did he lead him,
Washing his stains in the water like snow, his pelts, too, discarding,
So that the sea might bear them away; and his body appearéd
Fair; of his head he the fillet renewed, and himself in a mantle
Garb'd, as the clothes for his nakedness, such that or ever his city
Reach he, or ever he finish his journey, the mantle betray not

Age, but preserve all its freshness.
So into their vessel embarkéd
Gilgamesh, aye, and Ur-Shanabi, launching their craft on the billow,
They themselves riding aboard her.

(The magic gift of restored youth).

To Uta-Napishtim, the Distant ,
Spake then his wife: "Came Gilgamesh hither aweary with rowing,
What wilt thou give wherewith he return to his land?" and the meanwhile
Gilgamesh, lifting his pole, was pushing the boat at the seashore.
Then answer'd Uta-Napishtim to him, yea, to Gilgamesh spake he:
"Gilgamesh, hither didst come all aweary with rowing; O, tell me,
What shall I give thee as gift wherewith to return to thy country?
Gilgamesh, I will reveal thee a hidden matter . . . I'll tell thee:
There is a plant like a thorn with its root deep down in the ocean,
Like unto those of the briar in sooth its prickles will scratch thee,
Yet if thy hand reach this plant, thou'lt surely find life everlasting ."
Then, when Gilgamesh heard this, he loosen'd his girdle about him,
Bound heavy stones on his feet, which dragg'd him down to the sea-deeps,
Found he the plant; as he seized on the plant, lo, its prickles did scratch him.

Cut he the heavy stones from his feet that again it restore him
Unto its shore.

Gilgamesh spake to him, yea, to the boatman Ur-Shanabi this wise:
"Nay, but this plant is a plant of great wonder, Ur-Shanabi," said he,
"Whereby a man may attain his desire—I'll take it to Uruk,
Uruk, the high-wall'd, and give it to eat unto . . . . .
'Greybeard-who-turneth-to-man-in-his-prime' is its name and I'll eat it
I myself, that again I may come to my youthful condition."

(The Quest ends in Tragedy).

Broke they their fast at the fortieth hour: at the sixtieth rested.
Gilgamesh spied out a pool of cool water, and therein descending
Bathed in the water. But here was a serpent who snuff'd the plant's fragrance,
Darted he up from the water, and snatch'd the plant, uttering malison
As he drew back. Then Gilgamesh sate him, and burst into weeping.
Over his cheeks flow'd his tears: to the boatman Ur -Shanabi spake he
"Pr'ythee, for whom have toiléd mine arms, O Ur-Shanabi, tell me,
Pr'ythee, for whom hath my heart's blood been spent? yea, not for mine own self,
Have I the guerdon achieved; no, 'tis for an earth-lion only
Have I the guerdon secured—and now at the fortieth hour
Such an one reiveth it—O, when I open'd the sluice and . . .ed the attachment,
Aye, I noted the sign which to me was vouchsafed as a warning,
Would I had turn'd and abandon'd the boat at the marge of the ocean!"

Broke they their fast at the fortieth hour: at the sixtieth rested,
So in the end to the middle of Uruk, the high-wall'd, arrivéd.

(The Pride of the Architect).

Gilgamesh spake to him, yea, to the boatman Ur-Shanabi this wise:
"Do thou, Ur-Shanabi, go up and walk on the ramparts of Uruk,
Look on its base, and take heed of its bricks, if its bricks be not kiln-burnt,
Aye, and its ground-work be not bitumen, e'en seven courses,
One *shar* the city, and one *shar* the gardens, and one *shar* the 2
.... the Temple of Ishtar, amass'd I three *shar* and . . . of Uruk .

The Twelfth Tablet: Gilgamesh, in Despair, Enquires of the Dead

Column I.

(How the dead haunt the living).

Then, what time that the seine had pass'd through the Architect 's dwelling,
Aye, and the net had taken its toll . . . . said he:
"Lord, what is't I may do . . . .
Now, what time that the seine hath pass'd through the Architect's dwelling,
Aye and the net hath taken its toll . . . ."
Gilgamesh unto him spake . . . .
"If unto . . . .

(About two lines wanting, in which Gilgamesh presumably asks how the dead may be made to haunt the mourner).

"Gilgamesh, ..."

(The Mourner's Duty).

"If to the . . . thou drawest, unto the temple . . . .
Raiment clean shalt not don, but like to a townsman shalt . . . .
Nor with sweet oil from the cruse be anointed, lest at its fragrance
Round thee they gather: nor mayst thou set bow to the earth, lest around thee
Circle those shot by the bow; nor a stick in thy hand mayst thou carry,
Lest stricken ghosts should gibber against thee: nor shoe to thy footsole
Put on, nor make on the ground a loud echo: thy wife, whom thou lovest,
Kiss her thou mayst not, thy wife whom thou hatest—thou mayst not chastise her,
Aye, and thy child whom thou lovest not kiss, nor thy child whom thou hatest
Mayst not chastise, for the mourning of earth doth hold thee enthrallèd.

"She who dead lieth,
She who dead lieth,
Mother of Ninazu,
She who dead lieth,
No more with mantle are
Veil'd her fair shoulders,
No more her bosom

Drawn , like the lard cruse!"

Gilgamesh by contravening these customs attempts to raise Enkidu.

So did he draw the . . . to . . ., and came to the temples,
Put on clean raiment . . . and like to a townsman . . .
Aye, with sweet oil from the cruse was anointed: then at its fragrance
Round him they gather 'd: the bow did he set to the earth, and around him
Circled the spirits, yea, those who were shot by the bow at him gibber'd,
Carried a stick in his hand and the stricken ghosts at him gibber'd.
Put on a shoe to his foot-sole, and made on the ground a loud echo.
Kiss'd he his wife whom he lovéd, chastiséd his wife whom he hated,
Kiss'd he his child whom he lovéd, chastiséd his child whom he hated.
Aye, in good sooth, 'twas the mourning of earth which did hold him enthralléd:
"She who dead lieth,
She who dead lieth,
Mother of Ninazu,
She who dead lieth,
No more with mantle are
Veil'd her fair shoulders,
No more her bosom
Drawn, like the lard cruse."
Cried he for Enkidu out of the earth to ascend: "Not the Plague-god,
Namtar, hath seized him, nor fever, but only the earth: nor the Croucher,
Nergal, the ruthless, hath seized him, but only the earth: neither fell he
There where was battle of mortals; 'twas only the earth which hath seized him. "
So . . . for his servitor Enkidu sorrow'd the offspring of Nin-sun,

Aye, as he went all alone unto Ekur, the temple of Enlil:
"Enlil, my Father, 'tis now that the seine hath stricken me also,
Down to the earth—the net to the earth hath stricken me also.
Enkidu 'tis—whom I pray thee to raise from the earth—not the Plague-god,
Namtar, hath seized him, nor fever, but only the earth: nor the Croucher,
Nergal, the ruthless, hath seized shim, but only the earth: neither fell he
There where was battle of mortals: 'twas only the earth which hath seized him."
But no answer did Enlil, the father vouchsafe.
To the Moon-god he hied him :
"Moon-god, my Father, 'tis now that the seine hath stricken me also,
Down to the earth—the net to the earth hath stricken me also.
Enkidu 'tis—whom I pray thee to raise from the earths—not the Plague-god,
Namtar, hath seized him, nor fever, but only the earth: nor the Croucher,
Nergal, the ruthless, hath seized him, but only the earth: neither fell he
There where was battle of mortals: 'twas only the earth which hath seized him."

But no answer the Moon-god vouchsafed:
Then to Ea he hied him:
"Ea, my Father, 'tis now that the seine hath stricken me also,
Down to the earth—the net to the earth hath stricken me also.
Enkidu 'tis,—whom I pray thee to raise from the earth—not the Plague-god,
Namtar, hath seized him, nor fever, but only the earth: nor the Croucher,
Nergal, the ruthless, hath seized him, but only the earth: neither fell he
There where was battle of mortals: 'twas only the earth which hath seized him."
Ea, the father, gave ear and to Nergal, the warrior-hero,
Spake he: "O Nergal, O warrior-hero, give ear to my speaking!
Ope now, a hole in the earth, that the spirit of Enkidu, rising,
May from the earth issue forth, and so have speech with his brother."
Nergal, the warrior-hero, gave ear to the speaking of Ea,
Oped, then, a hole in the earth, and the spirit of Enkidu issued
Forth from the earth like a wind. They embraced and . . . . .
Communed together, mourning.
"Tell, O my friend, O tell, O my friend, O tell me, I pr'y thee,
What thou hast seen of the laws of the Underworld?" "Nay, then, O comrade;

I will not tell thee, yea, I will not tell thee—for, were I to tell thee,
What I have seen of the laws of the Underworld,—sit thee down weeping!"
"Then let me sit me down weeping."

The wretched lot of all who must die.

"So be it: the friend thou didst fondle
Thereby rejoicing thee—into his body, as though 'twere a mantle
Old, hath the worm made its entry: in sooth, then the bride thou didst fondle,
Thereby rejoicing thee—fill'd with the dust is her body . . . .
. . . . he hath spoken and into the"' ground is he sunken,
. . . he hath spoken and into the ground is he sunken."
"He who fell in . . . .
Didst thou see him?." "Aye, I saw . . . ."

        (About seventeen lines missing).

"As a pillar beautiful
Props? an inner portico . . .

        (About twenty-five lines missing).

"He who falleth from a pole
Didst thou see him? "Aye, I saw:
Straightway for . . . .
By removal of a plug . . . . . ."
"He whom death . . . .

"Didst thou see him?" "Aye I saw:
He's at rest upon a couch,
Limpid water doth he drink."
"Then, the hero slain in fight,
Didst thou see him?" "Aye I saw:
Father, mother raise his head,
O'er him wife in bitter woe."
"He whose corpse in desert lieth,
Hast thou seen him?" "Aye, I saw;
Not in earth doth rest his spirit."
"He whose ghost hath none to tend,
Didst thou see him?" "Aye, I saw,
Lees of cup, and broken bread
Thrown into the street he eateth."

THE END

Rosaries, Reading, Secrets: A Catholic Childhood in India
Anita Mathias
Benediction Books, 2022
368 pages
ISBN: 0955373700

Rosaries, Reading, Secrets is a lyrical account of Anita Mathias's turbulent Roman Catholic childhood in India. Mathias grew up in Jamshedpur, "The Steel City," a company town benevolently run by the Zoroastrians of Tata Steel. The Catholic church, run by American Jesuits, provided an all-encompassing world. In a pre-TV world, visiting friends was entertainment, juicy gossip flowed with homemade wine, and children sang, danced, and recited for guests.

Reading was a way of escaping volatile fights with her mother—fairy tales, Greek myths, Norse myths, Indian epics in children's editions and British children's classics. Libraries were a refuge.

Mathias, irrepressible and rebellious, known as the naughtiest girl in school, was expelled, aged nine, for disrupting classes with mischief, and was sent to a boarding school, St. Mary's Convent, Nainital, run by German nuns in the Himalayas. The virtual end of childhood—and a new adventure.

Wandering Between Two Worlds: Essays on Faith and Art
Anita Mathias
Benediction Books, 2007
152 pages
ISBN: 0955373700
In these wide-ranging lyrical essays, Anita Mathias writes, in lush, lovely prose, of her naughty Catholic childhood in Jamshedpur, India; her large, eccentric family in Mangalore, a sea-coast town converted by the Portuguese in the sixteenth century; her rebellion and atheism as a teenager in her Himalayan boarding school, run by German missionary nuns, St. Mary's Convent, Nainital; and her abrupt religious conversion after which she entered Mother Teresa's convent in Calcutta as a novice. Later rich, elegant essays explore the dualities of her life as a writer, mother, and Christian in the United States-- Domesticity and Art, Writing and Prayer, and the experience of being "an alien and stranger" as an immigrant in America, sensing the need for roots.

Francesco, Artist of Florence: The Man Who Gave Too Much
Anita Mathias
Benediction Books, 2014
52 pages full colour
ISBN: 978-1781394175

In this lavishly illustrated book by Anita Mathias, Francesco, artist of Florence, creates magic in pietre dure, inlaying precious stones in marble in life-like "paintings." While he works, placing lapis lazuli birds on clocks, and jade dragonflies on vases, he is purely happy. However, he must sell his art to support his family. Francesco, who is incorrigibly soft-hearted, cannot stand up to his haggling customers. He ends up almost giving away an exquisite jewellery box to Signora Farnese's bambina, who stands, captivated, gazing at a jade parrot nibbling a cherry. Signora Stallardi uses her daughter's wedding to cajole him into discounting his rainbowed marriage chest. His old friend Girolamo bullies him into letting him have the opulent table he hoped to sell to the Medici almost at cost. Carrara is raising the price of marble; the price of gems keeps rising. His wife is in despair. Francesco fears ruin.

* * *

Sitting in the church of Santa Maria Novella at Mass, very worried, Francesco hears the words of Christ. The lilies of the field and the birds of the air do not worry, yet their Heavenly Father looks after them. As He will look after us. He resolves not to worry. And as he repeats the prayer the Saviour taught us, Francesco resolves to forgive the friends and neighbours who repeatedly put their own interests above his. But can he forgive himself for his own weakness, as he waits for the eternal city of gold whose walls are made of jasper, whose gates are made of pearls, and whose foundations are sapphire, emerald, ruby and amethyst? There time and money shall be no more, the lion shall live with the lamb, and we shall dwell trustfully together. Francesco leaves Santa Maria Novella, resolving to trust the One who told him to live like the lilies and the birds, deciding to forgive those who haggled him into bad bargains--while making a little resolution for the future.

The Story of Dirk Willems: The Man who Died to Save his Enemy
Anita Mathias
Benediction Classics, 2019
18 pages, full colour
ISBN: 9781789430448

The religious wars of the Reformation had heroes and villains. There were giants like Luther and Calvin, and quieter unsung heroes. Five hundred years later, one of these stands out: the Dutch Anabaptist, Dirk Willems, who sacrificed his life to save his enemy.

www.ingramcontent.com/pod-product-compliance
Lightning Source LLC
Chambersburg PA
CBHW060612030426
42337CB00018B/3051